WILD CULTURE

SPECIMENS FROM
THE JOURNAL OF WILD CULTURE

EDITED BY WHITNEY SMITH AND
CHRISTOPHER LOWRY

DESIGNED BY BERNARD STOCKL

Somerville House Publishing
Toronto

Canadian Cataloguing in Publication Data
Main entry under title:
Wild Culture
ISBN 0-921051-62-X
I. Smith, Whitney (Whitney S.).
II. Lowry, Christopher (Christopher J.).
AC5.W55 1992   081 C92-093610-5

Designer: Bernard Stockl
Associate Designer: Lesia Olexandra
Assistant Editor: Alicia Peres
Photograph of the Editors: Jeremy Jones
Published by Somerville House Publishing,
a division of Somerville House Books Limited
3080 Yonge Street, Suite 5000
Toronto, Ontario M4N 3N1

Somerville House Publishing acknowledges the financial assistance of the Ontario Arts Council.

Thanks to CBC Enterprises for permission to edit and reprint *Ideas* documentary transcripts for *New Ideas in Ecology and Economics*, *Return of the Goddess*, *The Psychology of Fashion*, and *Delivering the Male*. Complete transcripts of these radio programmes are available for CDN $5 each from CBC Transcripts, Box 500, Station A, Toronto, Canada M5W 1E6.

Thanks to the Scottish Arts Council for permission to reprint *In Praise of Walking* by Thomas A. Clark from the exhibition catalogue, *The Unpainted Landscape*. Aerial photographs in *Northern Lights* courtesy of Her Majesty the Queen in Right of Canada, Department of Energy, Mines and Resources.

Some of Paul Dutton's additives have appeared in *Additives* (Toronto: imprimerie dromadaire, 1988).

Printed in Canada on recycled paper.

CONTENTS

EDITORIAL   1   **CALL OF THE WILD**
BY WHITNEY SMITH

CONVERSATIONS   3   **NEW IDEAS IN ECOLOGY AND ECONOMICS** BY DAVID CAYLEY
A wide-ranging investigation of the world as household

NUTSHELL   15   **R-TOYS-US?** BY BPNICHOL
Not like the angels I used to read about in the United Church Sunday Funnies

ESSAY   19   **HORMONES OR HISTORY?**
BY MARNI JACKSON
In matters of women's chemistry, it's a fine line between knowledge and superstition

APOCHRYPHAL REVIEW   29   **THE GREENING OF MADISON AVENUE**
BY STEVEN KLINE
Stunning revelations by a Finnish marketing-executive-turned-ethnonaturalist

INTERVIEW   33   **NATURE AND MADNESS**
PAUL SHEPARD WITH DAVID CAYLEY
A radical naturalist talks about the trouble with normal

WEAVE   47   **THE SWAN AND LEDA**
BY BRIAN FAWCETT
Yeats, Greek mythology and an innocent afternoon at the zoo

GARDENING   55   **EVERY PROSPECT PLEASES**
BY GARDENESQUE
Peacemaking between pets and plants

CUISINE   59   **HONOUR THY INGREDIENTS**
WITH MICHAEL STADTLANDER
AND CHRIS KLUGMAN
Two innovative chefs give tips on market research

POETRY   63   **THE OWLS AND DEPTH SOUNDING, LAKE WINDERMERE**
BY CHRISTOPHER DEWDNEY
Landscape readings from our resident paleoecologist

PATAPHYSICS   65   **NATURAL SELECTION**
BY RICHARD PURDY
'Pope Innocent XIII had a robe made of the skins of 85 of these frogs…'

DOCUMENTARY   71   **RETURN OF THE GODDESS**
BY MERLIN STONE
Her story

FORAGING   85   **WILD FOODS FIELD GUIDE**
BY DR. HANK HEDGES
A practical guide to picking some of the best wild edibles

READING   91   **CAMPING AT WALDEN POND**
BY CHRISTOPHER LOWRY
On a diet of bread, water, and ecstasy

MEDITATION   99   **IN PRAISE OF WALKING**
BY THOMAS A. CLARK
To be completely lost is a good thing

OBLIQUE ANGLE   103   **ENOUGH ABOUT THE PHALLUS!**
BY BRAHM EILEY
The scrotum gets its due

PROPOSAL   107   **NORTHERN LIGHTS**
BY PREMISES, TEXT BY JOHN FERGUSON
An ingenious plan

DOCUMENTARY   115   **DELIVERING THE MALE**
BY TIM WILSON
Robert Bly and James Hillman talk about courage, shame and sex

PARLOUR MUSIC   131   **LET'S TALK** BY PAUL DUTTON
Boogie woogie for telephone answering machine

DOCUMENTARY   133   **THE PSYCHOLOGY OF FASHION**
BY MARILYN POWELL
Gloria Steinem, Susan Brownmiller, Kennedy Fraser,
Gael Love and others on the emperor's clothes

SPEECH   147   **FILL IN THE BLANKS**
Better living through PR

STORY   151   **WHAT GOES AROUND**
BY SARAH SHEARD
'I was seized with a melancholia so sharp and physical,
its pangs felt almost sexual'

ESSAY   157   **THE BEER CAN OR THE HIGHWAY?**
BY DAVID CAYLEY
The problem of science is encoded in ecology

POETRY   165   **HEAVEN & HELL** BY SUE GELINAS
Orchids, lemon snaps, bàyonets, and a low
maintenance earth

SALON   175   **MIND JAZZ**
WITH WILLIAM IRWIN THOMPSON
'Preserving knowledge in an age of change or loss . . .'
A brilliant soloist plays his own brand of bebop

BEAUTY   195   **THE LANGUAGE OF SKIN CREAMS**
BY MARNI JACKSON
One woman's adventures in the skin trade

ALL SPECIES   199   **URBAN WILDLIFE**
BY MEREDITH ANDREW
Love thy neighbour—is there any other choice?

THE RANGER'S   205   **FEAR OF KNOWING IN MINNEAPOLIS**
TOWER   BY WHITNEY SMITH
'We murder to dissect'— Wordsworth

209   **BIOGRAPHIES**

GERA DILLON

CALL OF THE WILD

Ah, Humus! Humus!
From whom springs proud, unbridled awe and wonder,
Give us a quarterly . . . a pamphlet . . . a sheet . . . anything!
Upon which to imprint thy voice
On human grounds.

Speak, Humus! Speak!

OUR WALK THAT DAY took us over some pretty, rugged country.
'We don't want gardeners!' said our guide, squinting up at two
tangled evergreens. 'We've been in flowerbeds and animal hedges
in dreamland. We've been in commercial nurseries and even in
horticultural colleges! We just don't fit in!' He kicked a dead
stump with the toe of his boot. 'Of course, it could have been the
fertilizers. . .'

As we walked down the steep ridge, I happened to notice
something buried underneath a clump of raspberry canes. The
tiny purple thorns scratched the skin on my forearms as I reached
in to pull out the article.

'I think I've got something here!' I yelled, holding it up for the
others. Soon everyone was sticking their arms in through the
prickles and bringing out all sorts of things: essays, short stories,
interviews, drawings, a beautiful translation of Linnaeus' *Systema
naturae*. Someone even found a poem in a tree. But oh, the weeds!
There were so many of them! And there was no way we could get
at all the good material without cutting some of them down.

'You can't do that,' said the man from the Society. 'If you
have to cut the weeds down then either this isn't the right spot
or you aren't the right people.' We kept looking at the plot in
front of us and then finally the man sat down beside the stump

and picked up a stick, snapping it in two.

'In everything you come across there is always a choice. There's the choice of either going deeper, or going away. If you go deeper, you can go right into the thing until all you're seeing is yourself. *Fini!* Well, not *fini*—it's the start, really—but it can be any number of things: the yellow eyes of an owl at night, the dark wood in a wet meadow, the cracks in a salt desert, or the skin of a tree that compels you to touch it. Whatever it is, you get the memory, something personal, something lost and now—just now!—retrievable.'

He drew a line in the dirt.

'It's a starting point, you see.' He flipped the stick end over end down the hill. 'The rest is natural history . . . and the imagination.'

We stared at the ground for a while, then someone spoke.

'We're sure this is the right place . . .'

'Good! Good!' said the man, standing up with surprising ease. 'You won't be disappointed! There's a lot of room to grow here. And you know what they say—if it prints, grow it!'

The shadow of a cloud sailed over our heads and across the field.

'Well, I'll be off,' said the man as he started down the hill. 'You can find your way?'

'Yes, thank you,' I said, staring blankly at the odd assortment of things growing out of the weedy plot. ◉

NEW IDEAS IN ECOLOGY AND ECONOMICS

THE WORDS 'ecology' and 'economics' come from the same root: *oikos*, the Greek word for household. Ecology is the study of the household, economics the rules for running it. That's what the words say; but, in practice, our economy is more like an out-of-control machine that's rapidly reducing the household to ruins. We don't think of the Earth as a household at all. It's an 'externality', as the economists say, a source of the goodies we use, the 'out there' where we discard the parts we don't want.

Throughout recorded history, civilizations have declined as they used up the land on which they depended. Today, for the first time, civilization is becoming global. And this is forcing more and more people to become aware that devising an ecological economics is not a matter of choice. It's a matter of necessity.

As a radio producer for the Canadian Broadcasting Corporation's program, *Ideas*, I set out to find some of the people who are working to unite economics and ecology in a positive vision that goes beyond a merely defensive environmentalism. The result was four one-hour radio programs, called 'New Ideas in Economics and Ecology'. What follows is a series of excerpts from the transcript of that programme. The first concerns John Todd, a founder of the New Alchemy Institute on Cape Cod. Todd is a pioneer in the science of ecological design, and helped found an organization called Ocean Arks International to bring this science to the Third World, where it is most critically needed. Ocean Arks' first major project was the construction of a sail-powered fishing vessel designed specifically for Third World fishermen.

DETAIL FROM MATERIALISTIC DIALECTICS,
AMMUNITION ON PHOTOPAPER, BY GAR SMITH.

*They saw this as a liberation
technology, if you will, and they
didn't like the idea of a thousand
fishermen being able to go where
they wanted.*

OCEAN ARKS

JOHN TODD   We were aware, both through direct observation
and through FAO-United Nations reports, that literally millions
of fishermen in the last few years have been unable to fish, that
they no longer have the fuel for their outboards, the capital for
their gear, that this is a world-wide phenomenon, and that coast
communities are in really tough shape. And if you analyse why
they're in tough shape, it's because their countries' economies
have lost their buying power and their currencies have become
worthless. What happens when these currencies go soft is that the
infrastructure disappears: Mr. Yamaha outboard motor pulls out
(the local distributor doesn't have a hard currency, so he can't buy
it), and the oil importers don't want to import oil because no one's
going to pay for it with real money. So the economies come
unglued. We saw this happening all over the world at a terrifying
rate.

So one immediately says: Well, they could go back to the old
ways, they could build traditional boats and do it the way they did
it a generation earlier. But that argument breaks down when you
discover that the old ways involved boats being made of teak and
mahogany and rot-resistant woods. They'd all been cut down to
pay for the outboard motors and the steel boats and everything
else. The trees ain't there! That biological capital had been used
up. I started to ask myself this question: would it be possible to
build a boat that can be powered by the wind, that could be built
primarily out of fast-growing, soil-restoring weed trees, and that
would be as fast as the motorboats they were meant to replace?
Could we take the information of high-performance aircraft and
speedboats and apply that to the needs of artisanal fishermen?

DAVID CAYLEY   The answer to all this turned out to be yes.
With the help of a prominent naval architect, Dick Newick,
Ocean Arks came up with a vessel that they called an 'ocean

pickup.' A prototype, named *The Edith Muma,* was built in Dick Newick's boatyard, and launched in November of 1982. It was quite an event. James Morton, Dean of the Cathedral of St. John the Divine in New York, intoned a revised version of the traditional Anglican prayer for the launching of ships, the Paul Winter Consort played 'Amazing Grace,' and the *Edith Muma* set sail for Guyana.

The Guyanese fishermen were impressed. One even offered to buy her the first day out. But the *Edith Muma* was not for sale. She was the prototype, and the plan was to build more like her right in Guyana. It was there that things broke down.

JOHN TODD There was a lot of interest in Guyana in building a large fleet of several hundred of these, because one thing Guyana does have is marine resources. The financial community was interested in a technology transfer, but there were certain sectors, as I understand it, in the government that saw this as a *liberation* technology, and they didn't like the idea of perhaps a thousand fishermen being able to go anywhere they wanted. They didn't like the idea that they could sail up to Trinidad and pick up spare parts for the remaining outboards that were still functioning, or slip down to Surinam to get wheat flour and bring it back, because wheat flour was—I guess it still is—illegal. They were perfectly happy to control the movements of that sector of the society at the gas pump, and so the dominant sector in the government, which is, as you know, not a democracy, basically decided that this is not what they wanted.

GREEN DOLLARS VS. CASH

DAVID CAYLEY In Courtenay, British Columbia, I found an example of an alternative currency called LETS, short for Local Exchange Trading System. Its founder, Michael Linton, got the first glimmerings of this idea while he was listening to a talk by the late American philosopher, Alan Watts.

MICHAEL LINTON Alan Watts spoke at UBC about 20 years ago, to a student group mainly, about money. And what he said was that during the recession, the reason that things had slowed down and nothing was happening was that there wasn't enough

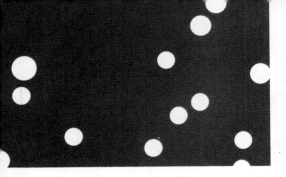

DETAIL FROM CAPITAL REVENUE,
MONEY ON PHOTOPAPER, BY GAR SMITH.

*Green dollars have two important
characteristics. First, they're
abundant: they can simply be
created at need; and second,
they're personal*

money around, which was quite right. He described in accurate and precise detail what happened, and he pointed out the absurdity of this. He said, 'Look, money is nothing more than a measure. It's like a foot or an inch or a metre or a kilogram. It's the thing we describe how much we've got of, not the thing itself. It's the thing we describe things with. And to say that we couldn't get on with our lives because there wasn't enough money around would be like saying we can't build this house today, we don't have any 'feet.' We've got the wood, we've got all the pieces, we just don't have the feet.

So I thought about that, and I thought, 'He's right, he's right.' But I didn't do anything about that because who could do anything about that? I mean, are you going to persude people you've got a different money system, that you could do it differently? I went and got a business degree, acquired a certain amount of experience in business, retail manufacturing, this, that and the other. I turned up in the Comox Valley and we've got unemployment. I certainly didn't have any way of earning a living in the conventional currency.

Then I heard about a small barter club, which was a group of people who wanted to connect with each other and swap things backward and forward because they had no money. So I went to a few of their meetings, and I found that there were some problems with direct barter, that you have to find two people who match up exactly with each other; and so quite often the only things that can be exchanged are rare parts of a person's life. The greatest part of their livelihood—food, maintenance, earnings—is not handled through those chance encounters with the person who's got exactly what you want and you've got exactly what they want. So in order to handle the matching of people's needs and requirements in this little group of people, I suggested that we put together a small notice board on which they could easily advertise what it was they wanted to offer or request. We would then keep a form of account of their mutual trading amongst each other for them in such a way that they had some idea of who was putting what in and taking what out—everything in balance. In other words, we would produce an internal money supply for the system.

DAVID CAYLEY   Today, the Courtney LETS system has more than 600 members. In the last three years, its volume of trade has amounted to about $300,000. I asked Michael Linton what I'd be getting myself into if I joined up.

MICHAEL LINTON   When you trade with somebody else in the LETS system, then part or all of that transaction can be acknowledged as a movement of 'dollars.' And of course these are not dollars issued by the Bank of Canada, they're just entries in a book of accounts. So some people have some green dollars to their name, and other people have a negative account of green dollars because they have spent some before they've earned some back. And it's just the interplay between people trading backward and forward that moves those so-called green dollars around and gives you the effect of having another money in your community.

DAVID CAYLEY   Green dollars have two important characteristics. First, they're abundant: they can simply be created at need; and second, they're personal: The people who issue them are personally committed to earning them back.

MICHAEL LINTON   Every dollar in the LETS system is backed by somebody's promise. That actually makes it the strongest currency in existence, principally because the person who makes the promise is always going to be able to redeem it. That is to say, he's around in the community, and the money he has promised is also around in the community, and he cannot fail to earn it back, if he's willing to do something—anything. Anything that anybody in the community wants; he could say, 'I'm available to mow your lawn for green dollars, look after your kids, consult in your business.' If it's something that somebody in the community conceivably wants and would have the money to spend on, they'll buy it. And you have put those green dollars into circulation so they're there. People will fulfill their own promises when the facility for them to do so is there, and that's the key distinction. With conventional money, people make promises and you can't believe a word of it.

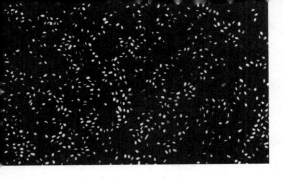

*With conventional money, people
make promises and you can't
believe a word of it.*

SARAH CALISTO   In the last few months, I have bought firewood for partial green dollars, say 50/50.

DAVID CAYLEY   Sarah Calisto is a Courteney resident and a LETS system member.

SARAH CALISTO   I have had a beautiful sweater knit for me and the wool spun. I gathered the wool from my dog, which I'd brushed out, and he's really a long-haired dog. One woman spun it and then I turned it over to another woman who then knit me a sweater out of it, and that was almost 100 percent green dollars. There's a natural foods store in Comox that takes 15 to 25 percent green dollars, depending on how he's doing with it that month. I go there often. In fact, I go there rather than shop in Courteney. I'll drive that five miles to Comox because he accepts green dollars.

DAVID CAYLEY   Is participation in this LETS system significantly reducing your need for cash, or is it just at the level now of sort of supplementing it here and there?

SARAH CALISTO   Yes, it's not reducing my need for cash because my main outlays are for my housing, my mortgage, my hydro, and my phone, and I can't use green dollars for those things. What this pays for is luxuries, extra things that I would not otherwise be able to afford.

DAVID CAYLEY   Sarah Calisto earns green dollars by sewing, selling things second hand, working in the LETS system office, and through child care. She's noticed that people use the system in several different ways.

SARAH CALISTO   The members seem to participate on maybe three different levels. One is people who are willing to accept 100 percent green dollars for anything. If you say, 'Can I give you green dollars because I don't have cash,' they say 'Sure.' And then there's another level, where people want a percentage of green, and a reasonable percentage of cash, say. They feel that they have to have a few dollars in cash to add to their income. And then there are other people who feel they'll do it for mostly cash and out of $100, they'll say 'oh, you can give me $5 of it in green'— which isn't really playing the game. It's as though they sort of want their foot in it, but they're scared. And of those people, I'd say that the ones who are willing to accept 100 percent green form a core of I'd say 150 out of 600-or-so members. And those people are trading around constantly with each other; the other ones are stepping out and interacting with those other members who aren't willing to do 100 percent once in awhile. But there's sort of a core group.

DAVID CAYLEY The Courteney LETS system is still in its infancy. Right now, only a handful of Comox Valley businesses will even accept green dollars. But if everyone accepted them, Mike Linton thinks that it could change the whole pattern of local economic development. At the moment, many communities are chronically short of cash. As a result, they're forced to rely on cheap imports because they're less expensive than things produced at home. But if communities had more money available for local trade, such as green dollars, then perhaps they could afford to make or grow some things they now import. The economic base would become more diverse, or stable and secure. There'd be more jobs. Communities could still engage in external trade, but they wouldn't have to stake their entire livelihoods on it. Altogether, Michael Linton has high hopes for the LETS system. He's invented a game called 'LETS Play' to teach other communities how to use it, and he's offering a software package for the system at cost. LETS systems are also being started in Vancouver, Toronto, and other North American cities. Meanwhile, Courteney is still learning to use its LETS system.

MICHAEL LINTON There are two directions one can go in a LETS system: one is earning green dollars and the other is spending green dollars. Consequently, there are two directions one cannot go in a LETS system: a person may be unable to spend them, or a person may be unable to earn them. Many people do not conceive they have anything to offer, so they are very reluctant to spend green dollars in case nobody wants anything they

*The 'real world' is supposed to be
harsh, mean and competitive,
nasty, brutish, and short…*

have. Others are more concerned with, 'What can I buy with this stuff?' For example, I've earned 500 green dollars, where can I spend it? They are often more problematic at this time, because people are geared to 'I earned some money and I want to be able to spend it now on the thing that is nearest my heart's desire'. That is to say, the B.C. telephone bill. B.C. Tel does not yet take green dollars. So there's often a situation where people are waiting for the article or service they want to buy to be available to them and regard the green dollar as not valuable or spendable until they see that article or service. Other people say to themselves, 'Well, what the hell, I'll have a cashmere sweater instead,' or, 'I will have back massages for the next six weeks.'

DAVID CAYLEY In other words, you let it enter your real life and say that you're going to live in the direction in which things are available to you in your community.

MICHAEL LINTON That's right, yes. Like Frank Sinatra's coming to town; so I go and see Frank Sinatra. I don't stand outside and bitch that it's not Bruce Springsteen. You know what I mean? You go to the show that's on.

BRIAR PATCH

DAVID CAYLEY A lot of what you've been reading so far is about a new economics, a social economics in which human interests and economic interests are not opposed to each other. It's an approach that offends many of our favourite prejudices about the 'real world,' which is supposed to be harsh, mean and competitive, nasty, brutish, and short. But according to Michael Phillips, these prejudices are just that—prejudices. Michael Phillips was once a vice-president of the Bank of California. Then, in the early '70s, he began to work as a consultant to many of the new hippie businesses that were then opening in San Francisco. There were whole foods stores, small publishers, craft stores, even a small circus called the Pickle Family Circus. These businesses were set up to do something, or share something—not just to make money—and the ideas of their owners were so much at variance with conventional business wisdom that many of them couldn't get a loan. That's where Phillips came in. He organized them into a mutual support network called the Briar Patch. In the process, Michael Phillips discarded his traditional ideas of business—that you have to be aggressive and competitive to succeed.

MICHAEL PHILLIPS What happened was that I did a sample of the 500 businesses, for which I had good records at that time dating back eight years. And of those 500 businesses, over 450 had started and been in business more than five years. The national average in the United States, Canada, and England is that 90 percent of businesses will have failed in the first three years. It's the difference between black and white, night and day. This group of hippies and young, naive people who didn't know what the traditional values were for business—and who had their own—were stepping into the same situation into which ordinary people would set foot and 90 percent of them would fail in three years. Five years later, 90 percent of them were successful. You'd have to say that what was right about the second group, and what was blatantly wrong about the first group, was the traditional way of doing business. And as I look back on it, that is what *honest business* is about. And that's what the Briar Patch made me realize.

DAVID CAYLEY Today, the Briar Patch has about 450 members in the San Francisco area. Membership is based on commitment to three basic principles.

MICHAEL PHILLIPS The values that Briar Patch businesses have as a whole are first, *openness*; second, *co-operation*; and third, the reason for being in business is *they love the particular business they are in*.

The openness was because of their attitude. They were the types of people we were dealing with, because one of the social values that was coming out of the late '60s was openness and honesty. If you were going to deal with people in a comfortable, long-term relationship, you had to be willing to listen to their

DETAIL FROM CARTEL FUTURES,
PHOTOGRAM, BY GAR SMITH.

*Michael Phillips discarded his
traditional ideas of business:
that you have to be aggressive and
competitive to succeed.*

feelings and their statements about you in order to create a genuine friendship. And that pervades Briar Patch business. They went so far that their financial statements are almost always available anywhere, you know, posted in the front of the store, posted in the business somewhere, on the front table. The openness was a value.

The second was that they actually had a genuine belief in cooperation, willingness to share their resources. One of the qualities about being in the Briar Patch and having the membership list is that you know that you can call other people on the list and they'll answer your questions.

And lastly was the value of being in a business they loved. Business is hard, and in order to make it through tough times you've got to love what you're doing. It just turns out, especially for small businesses, greed is insufficient motivation to keep people working late hours when there's a leak in the roof, when your spouse has run away with somebody that you're jealous of, your dog bit you, and your landlord has just sent you an eviction notice. And those things tend to happen in business, and they tend to happen late on a Saturday night. And just greed is not enough to get you to come back on Sunday morning, clean up the mess and begin dealing with the problems one by one. But loving the business might get you through it.

DAVID CAYLEY   Because of its success in San Francisco, the Briar Patch approach has now spread all the way to Japan and Sweden. The Swedes were so impressed by it that they adopted it as a model for national small-business development. Michael Phillips has been invited to Sweden several times to share his experience with Swedish businesspeople.

MICHAEL PHILLIPS   I visited a little town in Sweden called Philipstad. It's in the centre of Sweden, in Varmland. This was a town that was down to a little over 500 people. At one time it was a town of 25,000. And with a group of other people, I was invited to Philipstad to meet the businesspeople. There were about 30 people, and they'd all been asked to bring financial information about their businesses. They were very reluctant; but the person who invited them was important in the town, and at that point, everyone was willing to try anything. I said I don't know what good this is going to be, but I do know a lot about businesses, and if you give me a specific business I can give you a lot of very specific help. You show me the financial information, describe the business, and I can tell you how to improve your business. Who's going to have the first information? Well, nobody. No proper, self-respecting Swedish businessperson is going to show his or her financial statements, under any circumstances. They don't even talk to strangers, and even in a small town, they would never show it to anybody else. It's like showing your medical records to somebody else.

One woman who had a small woollen-goods store that appealed to tourists, said, 'Okay, here's my financial records. Can you see what I can do?' And so I projected them on the wall, and I started to ask her some questions and talk about it. Well, the room began to murmur and seethe and hiss with noise. And the noise just got louder and louder. Here I'm trying to talk to this woman about her business, and the noise level is getting louder and louder. Everybody was yelling and talking to everybody else, and the whole room was in pandemonium. They were yelling at her, they were running over to her, they were talking to her as fast as they could. And I'm standing on the sideline, and I ask my friends and the translator what's going on. They slowly translated the various things they heard. And they said, 'Here's one guy who said she's paying too much rent. He knows a place where she can get lower rent. There's another guy that said her transportation costs are too high. He goes into Stockholm every week, he'll pick up the stuff for her, his truck doesn't have that much in it when he comes back.' Everybody was offering her significant ways to reduce all of her costs and making connections for her with friends of theirs in different parts of the country who would buy her merchandise. They wanted to help her. When she was open and when they understood her business, which they did, they wanted to help her, and they knew how to help her.

Philipstad had a chance to apply its community spirit to the business at hand. It has been growing since then; I think there are 1500 to 2000 people living in the town, and the number of businesses has almost doubled in that period of time. The town changed direction.

Now there can be any explanation. Nothing else has changed about the environment. It's still the same trees and the same low-grade coal and the same fields with sugar beets growing out there. It's the fact that these people had the power to use their social skills in a new area of business. Instead of having all the resources in this teeny town isolated in financial terms, in terms of information and skills, they sort of formed one communal dinner. And in the same way, if everybody is eating dinner separately in their own homes, it's much more expensive than if you have a big potluck dinner to which everyone brings a little bit. That potential for community cooperation applies in business; but the first step is openness. Your financial records have to be open, and the potential miracles that flow from that are enormous.

How does it happen? Sociologists in the next century might come up with a good explanation. All I can see is that it increases social fabric, tightens the weave. And that's an analogy; it doesn't really say anything about what's actually happening. ◉

BARBARA KLUNDER

I HAVE NEVER **BEEN ONE** to get lathered at commerciali- zation aimed at children, or at least, the marketing of characters created to appeal to children. One look at Buster Brown shoes reminds us that the ghost of F.R. Oucault is still with us, though they haven't been publishing his comic strip since early on in this century. My only test is the thinking inside the fantasy world, the social setting in which the characters being marketed live. The Carebears, for instance, are an awful lot like the angels I used to read about in my United Church Sunday School funnies. And who can really object to a bunch of little ponies who run around being nice to each other? Isn't that what the Bobsey Twins did for years? I do start to worry, however, when the fantasy world includes, as Rainbow Brite's does, a race of happy beings who love working down in the mines bringing up the special sparkle stuff that allows the kids to put colour into their world. At that point I start waiting for the new character called Botha to start appearing in your neighbourhood toy store. If Toys-R-Us, then what are those toys saying about us?

We live in a time when still-developing social awarenesses definitely still lead to excesses. Obvious examples of this are the kinds of reverse cliches that go on. In a laudatory attempt to banish sexual stereotyping, female characters (be they bears, ponies, dogs, whatever) are never allowed to be pink, and male characters are never allowed to be blue. This is not necessarily because of advanced social awareness on the part of the people making the creative decisions but because they don't want to be accused of sexual stereotyping. But precisely because the focus is on what are finally the end products—the surface symptomology of deeper rooted problems—it's usually only the surface details that get changed. Rainbow Brite's world has an obvious debt to the world of Snow White with its dwarves mining diamonds, but the big difference is that the dwarves owned what *their* labour got them and Snow White became another worker in that world. It was her showing that she could pitch in and work alongside them that endeared her to the dwarves. In Rainbow Brite's world the dwarf/sprites do all the work, provide the comic relief and, though they do their bit when the going gets tough, it's usually Rainbow or one of the colour kids who pulls the fat out of the fire. Now you can be sure that there're no pink girl characters (though there is a Buddy Blue, a wonderful gay liberation name) and that characters who are of different colour all live together in harmony, but they do so in a world built on one race doing the labour while the other has the fun. Contrast this with the world of Strawberry Shortcake where the kids' job was to gather the berries from the garden. They had no one, or no thing, helping them. They did all the work themselves and they reaped the reward. And evil in that world was the Purple Pieman's attempt to gather fruit for his pies without doing the labour himself. Somehow that sounds more like it to me. It even had some wonderful twists. Somewhere along the road, Plum Pudding, who began life as a boy, turned into a girl. And nobody blinked an eye. That's definitely more like it.

Now having said all that, let me go on to say that part of the problem for a parent is that it's necessary to get into the fantasy world with the kid and muck about a bit. I don't know how many parents want to put in the time that that involves. Since children's play appears highly repetitive (though it's more 'insistent,' in the way Gertrude Stein used the term), adults tend to get easily bored. But getting in there with your kids is the only way you'll find out what's really going down. You have to dialogue with both your kid and the characters your kid is turned on to. I was in a toy store once watching the following scene go down:

A boy, about seven, wanted his mom to buy him some of the Transformers—high-powered robots that shoot it out with evil in the world of the future. This mom, clearly opposed to violence and, therefore, to violent toys, wouldn't, no matter how much the kid whined, screamed and pleaded. She was trying to buy him off with a Cabbage Patch Doll and, indeed, when they walked away the kid was carrying the doll while casting longing glances back toward the Transformers. I'll lay odds that when they got home the boy ripped the head off his Cabbage Patch Doll in a kind of orgy of violence the world has seldom seen. Because the problem is that Mom was doing her own kind of violence: she was getting between the kid and his chosen fantasy. I've never seen the approach that that parent took work. I'd be more inclined to get the boy the Transformer or the Rambo doll and then spend time in play changing the meaning of the whole thing, helping Rambo to behave in a more human fashion. Let him take up landscape painting or something that the kid is interested in. It's more fun and you find out things about what the doll or toy actually means to the kid, how it's incorporated into their world. Because every kid's incorporation of their play toys is unique.

Once again, violence as a solution is, among other things, a symptomology. Attempting to eradicate the symptom is its own kind of violence. The first trick is not to leap to conclusions but rather to get into what's happening and find out what the toy's meanings are from your kid's point of view, how he or she views and uses the character. Along the way you'll get an entire education. Sure there are high-powered moguls taking high-powered lunches to figure out high-powered strategies to get your kid to buy their toy. But once the toy is in the home you're in a position to work with its meaning because from then on it's out of their control. R-Toys-Us? I don't think so. Toys-R-Ours once they come home, but we have to work with them to make them our own. ◉

LAURA KIKAUKA'S ELECTRO-HOME

DAVID LAURENCE

HORMONES OR HISTORY?

BEHIND EVERY SCIENTIFIC THEORY that takes root in the popular imagination is the ghost of a superstition—something that makes people want to believe in the facts, even before they understand them. Right now biological determinism is riding high; everything from mood swings to serial murder is chalked up to 'chemistry,' the result of an extra chromosome, or too much testosterone. This has led me to several scientific theories of my own: it may be that 'nurture,' the whole centrifuge of environment, has spun so far beyond the control of any individual that it is simpler now to blame 'nature' for whatever we can't explain. And as far as women are concerned, we can blame hormones for a whole range of behaviour that may have nothing to do with chemistry at all.

All we have to do is to go back a bit in medical history to see that the line between fact and superstition has always been blurry. Each age develops a set of medical 'facts' about human behaviour that also operate as a cultural metaphor. In the nineteenth century, as Susan Sontag pointed out in her book Illness as Metaphor,

tuberculosis, or 'consumption,' was a fashionable sign of a sensitive, romantic nature. In this century, such 'female problems' as PMS, postnatal depression, and menopausal complaints have been diagnosed as everything from mild neuroses to sexist myths; now, in the eighties, they are the result of hormonal imbalances. But a hundred years from now, this emphasis on hormones as the cause and cure for whatever ails modern women may seem as quaint and misguided as the medieval theory of humours—with which hormones, as it turns out, have a lot in common.

In the Middle Ages, the four bodily fluids known as humours — bile, blood, phlegm, and spleen—were what determined a person's health and temperament. Like hormones, they influenced not just physical functions, but mood and personality. Too much phlegm, and a person grew sluggish and phlegmatic; for the overly 'sanguine' person with too much blood, the treatment was very simple—bleed the patient until the humours were back in balance again. With hormones, the theory is the same. If premenstrual problems are the result of deficient levels of progesterone (so the current theory goes), just add more progesterone and stir. With humours, as with hormones, everything was a potential symptom: stinginess, a tendency to weep, a dry cough, a hair-trigger temper—all were attributable to the waxing and waning of the body's fluids. Of course, the difference between the two is that hormones actually exist, and do influence mood and behaviour, whereas humours were more of a medical figure of speech. But the fact that a hormonal imbalance may be present in the case of PMS or postnatal blues, doesn't resolve the questions of cause and effect. What other factors—social, economic, cultural—might contribute to this hormonal unrest in the first place?

Although the name is new, the symptoms of PMS—that 'Iliad of Distempers peculiar to the Woman' as Galen called it— are at least as old as gynecology itself. Here is a case of 'suppressed menstruation' from the first English textbook, written in 1580:

> Signs and general indications of this sickness are these: aching and suffering with physical discomfort and a feeling of weight from the navel down to the privy member. . . such women have, at times, an unreasonable appetite for food not suited to them, such as coal or rinds or shells, and their complexion is a bad colour or grows pale.

And sometimes at this time they have a desire to consort with men, and so they do, and produce children that are lepers or have some other such evil sickness . . . and sometimes . . . it causes women to fall down in a faint as though they had the falling sickness. And they lie in that sickness for a day or two as though dead. And sometimes they have a dizziness with great confusion in the brain and think that everything is turned upside down . . .

Give or take a leper, this sounds like a classic case of PMS. The patient was suffering from a Plethora—too much blood—and her doctor would treat her disorder by bleeding her from the ankle. (Women on the whole were thought to be more 'moist' than men.) At least she had the comfort that medicine, such as it was, accepted the reality of her complaints. Twenty years ago, if a woman went to her doctor complaining of a 'great confusion in the brain' before her period, she would be treated, with more or less subtlety, as a neurotic. This opinion would be based on textbooks—still to be found on many doctors' shelves—that devoted many pages (and photos) to rare female disorders such as Hirsutism while dismissing 'premenstrual tension'—which 60 percent of women to some degree experience—in a paragraph or two, as 'psychological in origin.' And, oddly enough, modern feminists at first corroborated the view that PMS was 'all in the mind'—although for vastly different reasons.

As far as medicine was concerned, PMS was difficult to observe, or measure, or prove. It was simply a matter of believing what a woman said, a habit that few pre-sixties doctors bothered to develop. So medicine consigned PMS to the dark, murky depths of female behaviour itself. Then came the surge of feminist thought in the sixties and seventies. Eager to erase several thousand millenia of negativity toward female sexuality, feminists did not really want to admit to the reality of PMS; if women were seen as being different as a result of their menstrual cycle, they would inevitably be seen as defective—and unemployable. If men didn't have menstrual moods, then women damn well wouldn't either. It was too important to achieve economic equality with men to worry about these biological quibbles. And as a result, all the moods and malaise that went under the rubric 'premenstrual tension' were dismissed as another bad rap on women. Any discussion of biological differences between the sexes (other than the obvious) was tantamount to an attack on women, and a direct route to the old anatomy-is-destiny trap.

Then along came the cut-and-dried eighties, with their overwhelmingly pragmatic, material view of how everything from the economy to conception works. Happiness and health now seem to be strictly a matter of biochemical fitness: with the right vitamins, a little aerobics, and the appropriate hormone therapy, women can be as fit as fiddles, and predictable as men. Some of our most intense emotions, from euphoria to rage, can now be dismissed as hormonal hallucinations. Now, I have nothing against hormonal therapies, which undoubtedly rescue a lot of women from unnecessary depression and pain. But in our swing away from the psychological theories of the sixties, we may have gone too far in the other direction. It's time to bring a few cultural factors back into the picture, without losing sight of the biological facts.

Which, come to think of it, are worth refreshing, before we float away on the current of more theory. Before we go around blaming hormones for those brushfire domestic arguments, it might be worth defining them.

Both men and women have over a hundred hormones, which are chemical compounds produced by the endocrine glands, such as the thyroid, the pituitary, the ovaries, and the adrenals. Hormones are released into the bloodstream, which carries them throughout the body, but each hormone carries a chemical message that can only be 'tuned in' by a particular tissue or organ with the appropriate receptor site. In women, the hypothalamus in the brain dominates the menstrual cycle, affecting the pituitary and the ovaries, but the hypothalamus in turn is affected by two of the ovarian hormones—estrogen and progesterone. This circular system of signals and countersignals that passes between the brain and the reproductive system is known as a 'feedback loop.'

Even a thought or image can directly affect hormonal activity. A vivid example of this is the 'let-down' reflex in new mothers, when the sight or sound of her baby—even the image of one on TV—can cause a surge of the pituitary hormone prolactin, which signals the breastmilk to flow. If this is the case, it makes sense that other, more subtle cultural signals—including the value society places on the biological roles of women—might influence our hormonal lives as well. (This is where the facts end, and the theories creep in.)

In the body politic, social values act on the individual in the same way that hormones trigger physical changes. If the 'feedback loop' in our bodies is blocked or impaired, the intended function breaks down; this is how birth control pills are believed to work, by blocking the feedback pathway between ovaries and brain. In the same way, if the 'feedback loop' between women and society is negative—if, for example, the support signals for the role of motherhood are weak—then the result is a kind of hormonal imbalance in the culture itself: a world with too much testosterone and not enough estrogen. Our world, in other words.

It's easy to see how this state of affairs came about. In order to remain credible and effective in the Anti-Estrogen Era, every woman must, to some degree, betray her biology. (Any bad sport who doesn't want to be pregnant every ten months or so does this anyway.) She has to 'cure' or suppress whatever changes affect her before her period; she has to stay on top of the hormonal havoc of motherhood, if she takes that route, and she has to weather the radical transition of menopause—and she has to treat the emotions that accompany these female facts of life as unreal, mere 'mood disorders.' The whole notion of hormones as tricky little double agents allows women to isolate our purely biological functions as 'the enemy within.' Any suggestion that these transitions may actually be a source of strength, or creativity, or growth, is definitely suspect. After all, where did all that well-meant tampon-waving get us in the sixties? Nobody wants to campaign for corrective notions like Ovulation Euphoria or similar female jingoism. Still, I think our bodies are trying to tell us something, and that we have not been listening.

My theory is that women suffering from the 'hormonal imbalance' of PMS or postnatal blues are telling a kind of truth about the world we live in. They are expressing, in a tangible, physical sense, the degree to which female sexuality is still devalued and misunderstood. And by sexuality, I mean the whole continuum from menarche to menopause. My own prescription for this 'social disease' would be to send the whole culture to an Attitude Clinic, and to leave the premenstrual patient alone.

On the other hand, PMS is not a myth, and biochemistry is

certainly involved. But it is not a simple mechanical problem that can be cleared up with a dose of hormones—at least I don't think so. It seems to me that hormones have acquired the power of a modern superstition that views women as fine-tuned, delicately balanced, and essentially defective. Of course men share, in differing proportions, the same hormones as women, but because women lead a more dramatic hormonal life, either bleeding, breeding, or breastfeeding for some thirty-five years, they are readily seen as the victim of their hormones. Our consolation prize has been the validation of 'female problems' as real, live diseases—such as PMS.

Like personalized licence plates, PMS is a relatively recent phenomenon. Not long ago, it was referred to as 'premenstrual tension,' as if women were stringed instruments. Before that, PMS was just an indistinguishable part of the moodiness and misery that went along with being female. Now, we have a sleek medical acronym with an authentic sound, and special clinics for treatment. But in return for this new medical respectability we seem to have bought yet another distortion of what it means.

PMS is a real condition that has acquired the wrong name. The word 'syndrome' is misleading, since it simply means 'concurrent symptoms' and this suggests that any woman that gets irritable before her period has some kind of disease. The description 'premenstrual' also gives the impression that menstruation in some way cures PMS, or at least represents the resolution of the cycle.

But menstruation is strictly housecleaning; the real pivot in the menstrual cycle, when the hormonal tide turns, is ovulation. Thanks to the birth control pill and unenlightened sex education, for most women ovulation is strictly academic. You won't find many words wasted in high school health classes on ovulation. Instead, they watch animated films that show the demolition derby of conception, as the egg floats down the Fallopian tubes to collide with a gang of sperm.*

At this point it is tempting to talk about how menstruation is death-oriented, and how any culture in which girls know more

---

* EDITOR'S NOTE. THE SITUATION SEEMS TO BE IMPROVING. TWO SIXTEEN-YEAR-OLD GIRLS WE KNOW SAY THEY'RE OVULATION-WISE AND SO ARE THE BOYS IN THEIR CLASS.

about menstruation than ovulation is death-oriented too—how ovulation represents the time when the sexual power of the female, in the sense of its potential for life, is at its highest. However, given the praxis of the eighties, such talk would not only date me, but it might lump me in with the pro-life zealots, where I don't belong. But if—to return to the health class again—we take a closer look at the facts of the menstrual cycle, it might make more sense to redefine PMS as post-ovulatory, rather than prementrual. We could then talk about 'post-ovulatory blues' instead of 'PMS', which sounds like a new pesticide.

Stop me if you've heard this: roughly speaking, estrogen dominates the first half of the menstrual cycle, and progesterone the last. During the first fourteen days, one ovary or the other produces a little blister known as a follicle, which contains the ovum. Sometime around the fourteenth day, the level of estrogen decreases sharply, there is a surge of the luteinizing hormone LH, and the follicle bursts, releasing the ripe ovum. The follicle then forms the corpus luteum, which goes on secreting estrogen and increasing amounts of progesterone. Progesterone is the hormone that makes the breasts swell, and the uterine lining hospitable to the fertilized egg. But when conception doesn't happen, the corpus luteum degenerates, which lowers the supply of estrogen and progesterone to the uterus. At the same time, the blood supply to the womb begins to fluctuate, in what one researcher vividly termed the 'blush-blanche' phenomenon. Finally, the uterine lining breaks down and the resulting flow of blood and tissue is our boring old friend, menstruation. In the meantime, the ovarian hormones of estrogen and progesterone have been giving broad hints to the hypothalamus to repeat the whole cycle again. So, for another month, the female body begins the elaborate plot for pregnancy, as if IUDs and careers and the single child family had never been invented.

Hormonally, the body has no politics or five-year plan; every month it carries on as if having a baby once a year is a sensible idea. When this doesn't happen, as the hormones shift focus from conception to menstruation, the body may pass through a brief period of biological bereavement. Perhaps the premenstrual vulnerability and frustration that some women feel are completely appropriate to what is going on in the body—an echo of biological frustration. I sometimes wonder if it is our repression of these moods (chemical or otherwise) that leads to their more intrusive expression as anger, violence, depression, and all the other crippling aspects of 'post-ovulatory blues.'

I know how vaguely right-to-life that sounds, as if every woman were secretly a frustrated mother. This is not my point, but at the same time I find it hard to believe that our emotions and thoughts aren't affected by such a momentous reorientation in our bodies. Recognition of this mild sadness between ovulation and menstruation wouldn't have to mean that a woman 'subconsciously' yearns for children, or has to choose between procreation and depression. It would simply be an anticipated shift in the quality of emotions. If we had a reference point for these unreasoning feelings of loss or vulnerability, we might not go looking for people—or hormones—to blame.

Instead, many women aspire to the straight line of the male hormonal graph, with its emphasis on emotional consistency. Whether or not this model of masculine stability is true, society seems to believe it is. In the case of really severe PMS, the female body may be throwing a tantrum because what it says—what it means—is being ignored. It is one thing to control female fertility—a freedom most of us welcome—but it is another to ignore it altogether.

AM I SUGGESTING fertility dances and black armbands in memory of the widowed ovum? Special sections in restaurants for the post-ovulatory female? Not quite. But there is evidence that, regardless of the treatment given, PMS improves with recognition. Researchers have been puzzled by the fact that, although studies show that progesterone can be used successfully to treat PMS, control groups have benefited almost as much from placebos. To some scientists this is more evidence that PMS is 'all in the mind,' but it also proves that any form of validation is better than none. In fact, it may be the 'psychological' component of PMS that is culturally induced—the result of the stress of coping with mood changes, keeping them under wraps at work, and worrying that it is really just neurosis.

Think what might happen if the culture as a whole reversed its values in a way that approved of female hormonal rhythms—

women would not be called 'irrational' before their periods, but 'emotionally responsive.' Postnatal blues would be seen for what it usually is—a case of Cultural Neglect exacerbated by simple fatigue and ricocheting hormones.

Instead, what we have is a double-barreled negativity: the traditional devaluing of motherhood, and the stubborn feminist fear that any sort of biological identification will force women back into dead-end roles. Once you admit to hormonal differences, the old logic goes, the spectre of the Premenstrual President arises, with her fickle finger on the nuclear-war console. Women now need to reassert their biological differences from men as strengths, not weaknesses.

Lately, a revival of the cult of motherhood has made pregnancy and childbirth voguish, but deep down the values remain unchanged. Career women still take pains not to be affected by their periods or their pregnancies. And if they have a baby, they hustle back to the office after three months before they lose their place in line. The huge, important job of having children is still that form of cultural exile known, quite accurately, as 'maternal leave of absence.'

But if pregnancy and child care became one of life's executive positions; if we educated the young in the power of female fertility as well as the perils of sexuality; if nursing mothers were paid $42,000 a year . . . well, dream on. Until that happens, we blame hormones, not history. And the result is this—once again: it is not history that changes, but those paragons of flexibility, women. If pioneer women could build and bake and give birth and shoot bears, then the pioneering working woman can overextend herself too, composing office memos in her head while she breastfeeds the baby.

Meanwhile, we take our persistent 'female problems' to a clinic, or a shrink, as if our bodies were somehow betraying us, instead of the other way around.   ◉

It was the secret doctrine of a Madison Avenue cabal laying down the foundation of a conspiracy more secretive than a Mason's handshake.

THE GREENING OF
MADISON AVENUE

The Greening of Madison Avenue: Advertising and the Subliminal Landscape, by Enilk Nevets (Boulder: Pavlovian Press, 1986), translated by Karal Togram; 348 pp., paper, $18.50.

WE HAVE LONG SUSPECTED that the total destruction of nature would be the logical consequence of modern technological progress. What few of us realize is that since 1930 a small, dedicated coterie of concerned environmentalists has been pursuing a subtle strategy of preservation on a global scale. This underground movement has been composed of none other than the top seven advertising executives of the 20th century.

If this sounds like hogwash to you, then you should have a look at a remarkable new book by a Finnish marketing-executive-turned-ethnonaturalist, Enilk Nevets, called *The Greening of Madison Avenue: Advertising and the Subliminal Landscape*. Nevets claims to have discovered one of the best-kept secrets of the 20th century. If he's right, he holds the key to our understanding of the immense power of the media to penetrate the farthest reaches of our unconscious minds.

This lavishly illustrated book is both a personal voyage of discovery and one of the most impressive pieces of academic gumshoeing we have witnessed. Formerly a Helsinki adman himself, Nevets uncovered the first clue to the Madison Avenue cabal while comparing consumers' comparative short-term memory retention for two competing hair products. In his own words, 'I was fascinated, dumb-struck! How was I to explain the absurdity of the connection I saw before me? It made no sense that advertisers would use a natural landscape simulating a close-up of a scalp to

explain the effectiveness of a hair-colouring product. Unless I looked at the ad again: "I am Sand." Blonde colours are found in nature. The extraordinary memory-retention power of this ad could only be explained by something deeper, a subliminal message. The barren landscape emblazoned on the unconscious a powerful natural icon. Then it struck me. They weren't selling hair colour at all! They were selling *wilderness*....'

Nevets followed this line of investigation and quickly discovered that a majority of advertising appeals were based on images of nature, and that over 35 percent of all ads have subliminal natural images in them. This was the first step toward solving the case. Where others found sexism, Nevets found nature.

He realized that 'advertising was increasingly becoming the only place where modern man could have contact with nature. Advertising was the modern equivalent of a Gainsborough landscape painting, a botanical garden, and a zoo all rolled into one.'

Because Nevets could not explain the adman's fascination with nature on rational grounds related to product sales, he began to look for other explanations. He had to dig deeper to identify when and how the 'greening of advertising' began. Buried in a *Fortune* magazine of the late 1930s, he discovered the ad that broke the case. It seemed straightforward until Nevets viewed it in a mirror and discovered the equation 'Capitalism = Cow' reversed: 'Cow = Capitalism'! To Enilk Nevets, the hieroglyphics made sense. This was not a simple-minded statement by the second-largest ad agency of the thirties. It was the secret doctrine of a Madison Avenue cabal laying down the foundation of a conspiracy more secretive than a Mason's handshake.

Subsequent research revealed this first decoding to be correct. In 1927 in a small restaurant in the South Bronx, seven top advertising executives, including J.B. Watson of the JWT agency,

Albert Lasker, and Bruce Barton of an agency later to become BBDO, met not as rivals but as dedicated conservationists and animal lovers. Their positions at the hub of American free enterprise had left them with serious concerns about the future of American society and the natural world. Secret minutes from

This is a Cow. The cow is the mother of capitalism. Capital means "head." Capitalism was originally a count of heads of cattle.

Here is an Ox, a son of our Cow. He was the first machine, the origin of power . . . which is merely Nature harnessed and put to work.

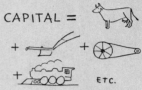

CAPITAL = + + ETC.

CAPITAL IS CATTLE and their derivatives. It is our whole machinery of production and distribution—plow, treadmill, harnessed power.

A PRIMER OF CAPITALISM

Many of us think of economics as an abstract theory . . . something visionary and academic. But isn't it just a study of *people trying to make a living* . . . trying to get

"MORE FOR THE MONEY"?

"WE seem to need a common ground, a common agreement about some very simple fundamentals of economics. There is no reason why a company president, a union-labor leader, a youngster learning his first job and the congressman representing them all should not agree on these. Each has his living to make and each is dependent on the others in making it.

"Capitalism—private and state—has an important bearing on our efforts to make a living. Some people seem to have the idea that they can take it or leave it, according to the whim of the moment. But perhaps capitalism is something more than just another 'ism,' which we can put on or put off at will.

"This little booklet is an effort to find out. With plain words, simple drawings and a human viewpoint—exactly the same method used in the best advertising to interpret products and institutions to the public—it seeks to interpret private and state capitalism as they exist today."

* * *

The above paragraphs are taken from the foreword to the *Primer of Capitalism, Illustrated*. Those who must deal with public opinion as it affects American business may find the technique of this new Primer interesting. Like the *"Brookings Primer of Progress"* —now in its fifth edition, the Primer of Capitalism will be sent free upon request. Address: 420 Lexington Avenue, New York, N. Y.

J. Walter Thompson Company

NEW YORK   CHICAGO   SAN FRANCISCO   LOS ANGELES   ST. LOUIS   SEATTLE   ·   MONTREAL
TORONTO   ·   LONDON   PARIS   ANTWERP   THE HAGUE   BUCHAREST   ·   BUENOS AIRES   SÃO PAULO
CAPE TOWN   ·   BOMBAY   ·   SYDNEY   ·   LATIN-AMERICAN AND FAR EASTERN DIVISION

EVERY NATION is a mixture of state capitalism and private capitalism. Under the American system these two are not enemies, but working partners.

FOUR MILKMEN to each cow will not produce any more milk. Sharing a given amount of work does not produce any more wealth—or result in a higher standard of living.

A FAIR PROFIT for capital . . . a fair wage to workers . . . a fair price, continually lowered to create more consumers—this is the true aim of private capitalism, proven in actual practice —the aim of More for the Money.

TROPICAL BLEND
FOR THE SAVAGE TAN

This is the darkest tan ever. And you get it fast with Tropical Blend, by Coppertone. It smells like fresh coconuts. And it has strange tropical oils. It lets the sun tan you wild. Unleash the savage tan with Tropical Blend. Then watch. The natives will get very restless.

TROPICAL BLEND BY COPPERTONE

that first historic meeting reveal that it was Watson who proposed the plan. 'Destruction of the natural world, the paving of Paradise, is the logical outcome of Progress,' he said. 'Forests will be cut down, wilderness will be no more, and the laboratory will become one of the last remaining habitats for animals.' Zoos and parks would not suffice to preserve the basic elements of the natural world. A grander design was necessary. He lowered his gruff voice and uttered these immortal words: 'Gentlemen, he said, advertising must become the symbolic repository of nature. When all the rivers are industrial waste and the trees are made of plastic, advertising will be the bulwark of the things we treasure.'

And so the conspiracy began. Lasker launched the *Camel* and *Black Cat* cigarette campaigns the next year. JWT brought out a *Maxwell House* coffee ad based on a Stubbs painting. The surge of animal-inspired products and ads grew. Cars echoed the wildlife of the Western plains in their names—jaguars, mustangs, pintos, impalas, and cougars bounded across our TV screens chased by the Esso tiger trying to leap into their gas tanks. Cigarettes were never puffed in stuffy bars and smelly offices, but by rugged cowboys or athletic couples beside rivers redolent with the promise of spring.

Every page of Nevets's book reflects the growing commitment of the advertising industry to what he calls 'the impregnation of the unconscious mind with the vital imagery of the natural world, building an enduring bastion of collective memory which will endure as long as humanity itself.'

NATURE AND MADNESS

Defining a 2000-year-old neurosis
for David Cayley

THE NORWEGIAN PHILOSOPHER Arne Naess illustrates the pitfalls of environmentalism with a parable. He says we are standing on the banks of a polluted river desperately trying to remove the pollutants without ever directing attention upstream to find out where they came from in the first place. Naess calls the attempt to get beyond the symptoms to the source 'deep ecology.' Not everyone involved in this quest accepts the label, but a growing number of thinkers claim that only a cultural and conceptual revolution can restore our right relationship to nature. They say that even the words we use may betray us: that the very word environment still implies something definitively separate from us, which acquires value only in relationship to human beings.

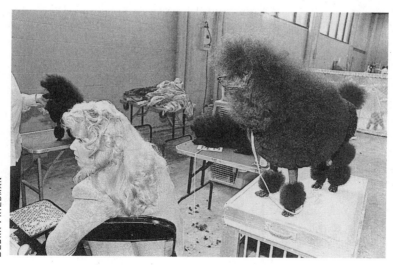

DEBRA FRIEDMAN

One of the most interesting and influential of these thinkers has been Paul Shepard, a teacher at Pitzer College in Claremont, California, and the author of a series of books that have probed the relationship between nature and civilization. When I met him at a friend's apartment in Oakland, I had just finished reading his book *Nature and Madness*. It was the ideas in this book that I wanted to discuss with him. He began by describing his search for a basis on which to build a new relationship with nature.

SHEPARD In my graduate work I was committed to the notion that an aesthetic appreciation of nature can counterbalance the purely materialistic and economic approach from which we get the notion of natural resources and resource management. But I was disillusioned, largely by the geographer David Lowenthal, whose attacks on the idea of wilderness were powerful enough to convince me that if we allow our feeling for the natural world to rest on an aesthetic basis, then we are likely to lose it—because tastes change. It was his observation that nobody cared much for wilderness three hundred years ago. This notion of the 'beauty' of wilderness is a very recent thing.

I began to read anthropology in the hope of finding a sounder base from which to begin my own work. At that time there was a lot of new work coming in from the study of tribal peoples. We had for the first time good solid studies, in the field, of still-living, foraging, hunting and gathering, non-agricultural people, which gave us a new sense of the value of the views of such people. The thing that astonished me most was not that there was a good, harmonious, ecological relationship among such people and their surroundings, but that their intellectuality about animals was so sophisticated, and that their culture contained such erudition.

Claude Lévi-Strauss spoke of Australian aborigines as 'intellectual snobs' after spending an evening with them talking about their mythology. I was deeply moved by this idea that we are not dealing with people who have merely vague and general notions about their world, rather, they highly evolved stories in which their profound heritage of observation and thought makes connection to the natural world. Lévi-Strauss has called this 'totemism,' which is a kind of poetic view of nature as it might imply social groupings and social actions. So that's where I took a ninety-degree turn in my own thinking.

Not only did I find that the way in which the natural world was dealt with involved the most intense objective observation, at the same time with a theological bent to it, but that such tribal peoples reared their children in the most extraordinary way. By the time the child was initiated into an adult society, that child had a sense of being at home in the world, of being a part of things, of living in a world that was good, with a great deal of respect for non-human beings—what we would perhaps call a kind of humility about the natural world. Being a biologist, my own bias was to speculate that hundreds—perhaps thousands—of generations living a tribal existence had built into our own bodies—our own genetic makeup—certain expectations about what life would be like for us as infants, and as children, and as adolescents; that the body and the mind had a program of assumptions about the way in which we would be dealt with by parents, by peers, by elders, and so on, that involved certain critical period experiences. So what seemed to be common among this diverse group of foraging peoples was certain kinds of experiences in infancy and childhood which one might call bondings, not only to mother and parents and people, but to the landscape and to the natural world, and then certain experiences that involved a religious perspective, and involved initiatory ceremonies, and experiences that the adolescent went through that moved the individual to a more mature perspective on himself or herself in the world as a whole.

CAYLEY You've said in *Nature and Madness* that you've come to regard this primal form of human development as more 'normal' than what we are used to, and I wonder how you can argue that it's more normal.

SHEPARD The unfolding of one's being is intimately and continuously connected with certain kinds of inputs, certain kinds of experiences, and if these don't happen, then we fall into a kind of frustration the result of which is that we autistically create these experiences as best we can. For instance, if we have inadequate bonding to a mother, maybe we cling throughout our lives to pets, or if we are not appropriately introduced into a cosmic view of the world through instruction by an uncle, or by a group of elders, perhaps we fall into the gang situation, in which we create an artificial heritage of ideas and initiations, and sufferings and brotherhoods and perspectives. So I can only defend the notion by a kind of analogy to other developmental processes that go on in our bodies. The acquisition of language, it seems to me, is intimately associated with learning the names of things, especially plants and animals, and the games that children play clearly include, in most societies, the imitation of animals, which helps them to establish a sense of similarity to and yet difference from those creatures.

It's a very difficult idea to really conclusively prove, but every day and every month we get increasing evidence that there is a normal and an appropriate way to grow up that involves not only good mothering, but imprinted childhood landscapes, and a rich experience of the non-human life in one's vicinity.

CAYLEY   What is this evidence?

SHEPARD   The evidence is all around us. The thing that got me into 'nature and madness' was this: we now have an enormous amount of information on how the biosphere works, and how ecosystems work, so why are these systems being ravaged, nonetheless? Obviously, merely that information is not enough. I thought, in my young adulthood as a teacher, that if we merely spread the information, people would do the right thing. But obviously, that's not the case. We are no better off with respect to the way we're dealing with the natural world and the environment today than we were 25 or 50 or 100 years ago. Why is it? Something obviously is wrong with how we have dealt with this information. We have assumed that we are rational beings that would, through political and administrative means, take the proper measures. We're not doing this. We're losing a species a day through extinction. In fifteen years we will be losing an animal species every hour. We only have to look at what's happening to planet Earth now—to the forests, the tropics, the forests of equatorial regions around the world, to life in the seas, to our grasslands. We're still removing non-human life, destroying the soil, and overpopulating the world. So I come back to the question, 'What is it that's involved here?' And it seems that no matter what tribal people you look at where children have certain kinds of experi-

ences, that those people, although they develop very different mythic and ceremonial and storied explanations of their relationship to nature, for the most part live in a fairly good balance with their natural world. What we're talking about is something that happens in those first fifteen years of a person's life.

CAYLEY The presumption that there is a 'normal' or a proper course of development is, in our society, one that is usually met with hostility. It speaks against what I think is the quintessentially modern view that our essence is freedom, that our essence is change, and that therefore we are a being that is completely open.

SHEPARD Of course, and you have only to look at the last 300 years of Western philosophy and science to see where this comes from. We have the notion that we are essentially beings who can create ourselves, and whose freedom is limited only by our imagination. So biological determinations or limitations of this kind are not going to be welcomed and are simply not going to be allowed expression where decisions are being made. It's clear in the discussion of human genetics, that in spite of the growing evidence linking human pathology to genetic potential—genetic limitations—we're extremely slow in admitting this possibility. And modern psychology, of course, has been committed to the view that we are largely what we learn to be or teach ourselves to be.

CAYLEY And I think that there's furthermore a feeling, particularly on the political left, that any argument which presumes that there is a normal course of development, that makes arguments from biology, is certainly conservative if not cryptofascist.

SHEPARD   I find that all the time. The liberal-conservative, left-right distinction in connection with the whole of ecological and environmental thought is extremely interesting. I remember how surprised I was as a graduate student that it was the conservatives who were the great destroyers—and I'm thinking of the great land owners, the lumber barons, the cattle barons and so on—and how astonished I was that the word 'conservative' would be used for people who were most ready to tear up the environment, and so I expected on the other hand that the left and the liberal view was the one to which my own studies led. But as you have said, it has its own problems with admitting that we are a limited kind of species, as are all of the other species on the planet.

CAYLEY   Where do you locate the beginning of this conflict between humanity and nature?

SHEPARD   I think that it begins well before civilization, if you define civilization as the first cities, as the first civilized life, and the wheel, and writing, and all that. It's not very fashionable to attack the whole idea of agriculture, of farming, at a time when life in cities makes a pastoral view of the world so attractive; yet if I had to pick a moment in human time when what the Christians call the Fall took place, I think it would have to be with that subversion of ecosystems in which we took other species into slavery, into captivity. The taking of substantial numbers of wild creatures and turning them genetically into monsters which were totally dependent on their human caretakers had some extraordinary effects on our own psychology. What it did was to create a world around us which we had made, and over which we had control. Now we have a thousand generations of human beings who have grown up in that world which seems to have been made by the will and the creativity of human beings, in which the most important creatures are those extraordinary blobs—and I can't help but use this word, because what we do to an animal, when we modify it in domestication, is to deprive it of all of its subtlety, of the richness of behaviour and form which its natural ancestors had. The result is change in our own perception of nature. Nature then becomes brutish, it becomes simple; it becomes something which we must manage. We are to be the stewards, the caretakers of the world. We are to take responsibility for the world. Which merely says that we are on the way to making slaves of the rest of creation, or bringing it to extinction.

The Fall took place, if there was such a thing, when we became settled people with a very impoverished fauna and flora around us.

CAYLEY In *Nature and Madness* there is a chapter called 'The Desert Fathers.' This was one of the most intriguing parts for me—this idea of the ancient Hebrews occupying a crack in the dialectic of city and settled agriculture, the pastoralists occupying a crack from which so much of Western religion and civilization is generated.

SHEPARD Up until the time, at least of the early Semitic peoples, there was always an idea of sacred powers which were seen as governing the planet and its processes. They were incarnate, they were manifested in all kinds of natural forms, and the creatures themselves had some aspect of this divinity or sacredness. But these tribal peoples, moving on the edges of the desert— not totally committed to cities, not totally committed to Arabic pastoralism—became sufficiently detached about themselves and their circumstances that they could begin to speak of themselves in a new way. They could begin to see themselves outside of the groups of people around them who were committed to earth deities. Such peoples came up with the wholly new idea that divinity was not manifest and embodied around them, but was at some distance and was not immediately approachable through appeal.

What has been passed on to us is this incredible sense of the distance of an all-powerful and increasingly singular deity who could not be appealed to through ordinary ritual. They removed from the surface of the earth and from our immediate environment that sacred quality which had been there for as long as we had been on Earth. I think for them the fact that the Earth had been created by God meant that it still had a certain quality of the sacred about it; but the consequences of this for the last two-and-a-half thousand years have been the notion that the Earth and its creatures are merely material or merely physical beings without sacredness. It was the removal of the ceremonies involving the natural world from adolescent initiation that amputated from the experience of every child that final formulation of a cosmos in which the natural world played an important, dynamic role.

CAYLEY But isn't our emergence from nature a necessary part of the evolution of consciousness, a necessary part of human self-discovery?

SHEPARD I have a colleague called John Cobb, a Whiteheadean theologian who has an incredible interest in environmental matters. We teach a course together in which we play this back and forth. Cobb is always ready to call my attention to the fact that I couldn't be talking about my culture and history in this way had I not come through this peculiar Hebrew and Christian history that I have come through. Your suggestion, therefore, is true. There must be a third possibility. Having gone through the Fall we are now removed from our commitment to a culture totally imbedded in a given ecological system. We cannot recover that past without some unbelievable catastrophe. Neither can we keep on distancing ourselves in the way that I see a purely scientific process would lead us to do—increasingly objective about the world, and increasingly depriving that part of ourselves which needs and hungers for a cosmic and a theological commitment. So we need a new approach. We must go on now to the recovery of those things which are essential to human growth, maturity and development, that lead to a sense of what Owen Barfield called 'participatory concern' with the world, but we have to do it deliberately and consciously. To what extent one can deliberately create a mythology, a culture—I cannot say.

CAYLEY What are the essential elements in a hunting and gathering way of growing up that you think are still accessible to us?

SHEPARD I think the essential things are already visible in the studies of childhood that have been made. The difficulty is that, in spite of the care with which we have been studying children, the people who have been doing it have not been very interested in nature, the non-human part of the world. We have this tremendous amount of information, but the interpretations usually neglect even the possibility that some of what we're seeing in-

DEBRA FRIEDMAN

volves some special kind of experience with the non-human.

For example, in the last ten years, the studies of infant-mother bonding have led to a whole new sense of the importance of the naturalness of the nursing mother. The importance of contact, of sound, of the smell of the mother, the taste of the milk, of the amount of time that the infant spends with its mother. It seems to be essential for the rest of the child's and the adult's behaviour for it to come into a world with confidence that there is a protective, informing partner who is nourishing and who is beautiful and who is there. What we then go on to do is to assume that what the young child does with this is to grow into a totally human context. Yet we have all this information on children in places and children in play which suggests that what they are in fact doing is transferring the features of that infant-mother bond to some kind of larger matrix; that is, in the third to tenth year of childhood, there is a kind of attachment to 'places' apparent in the everyday lives of children. These places are somehow imprinted after the model of the mother, as protective, as interesting, as communicating, as nourishing, and infinitely challenging in terms of exploring these bonds. The child's bonding with place is creating in the child the terms which will serve as metaphors, as images in the poetic language for creating a total universe, a cosmos, when he or she comes to adolescence. How else do we talk about ultimate things? When we talk about Paradise we talk about a landscape which looks like a pastoral garden. All of the ultimate imagery of what we believe to be finally possible and true about the universe requires a language or other signs or images that come back to social and ecological relationships formed in infancy and childhood.

CAYLEY What about adolescence and initiation? It seems to me that the inability to become an adult, the fact that this society provides no means to become an adult, is a very important social pathology. How do you see this?

SHEPARD What continues to astonish me is that great and important scholars on the subject of development and on religious history, people like Ernst Cassirer, or Mircea Eliade, all talk about what they see as the importance of that crucial time of adolescence. The time involving a great hunger to be separated from one's parents, to follow, as it were, lessons learned from an uncle or friend of the family or some other elder; a preparedness to go through suffering with a group of one's peers; and especially that yearning for religious instruction, for information about ultimate questions. So we have this almost incredible metamorphosis from the child of ten, who cares nothing about such things and who's not very interested in poetry, to the pubescent person who begins to write poetry and tell bad puns and be interested in language—the way words can mean two things at once—and the way we have to use language to talk about God. We are so deeply committed in modern civilized society to the belief that we can make ourselves that we ignore all the implications of not understanding what's necessary for the development of the heart and mind of the adolescent: that they are so clear about and desirous of undergoing the suffering, losses, and deprivations that instruction implies. We don't do anything about that. We have given up. We have lost the traditions that earlier on provided the ritual and ceremony of rebirth—except in native North American communities where tribal peoples still have a cultural life. It could be that one of the things that's happening in North America is that those descended from white Europeans are now beginning to understand that there may be a great deal to learn from these existing tribal cultures.

CAYLEY   What are the consequences of an absence of these bondings to nature? What would be the positive consequences if they were present?

SHEPARD   Modern psychiatry is full of speculation on the failure of mother-infant bonding. One of the things that comes out of this failed connection is identity problems, and problems of relating to the 'other'. The kinds of psychotic and psychopathic behaviour which psychiatry relates to failure of bonding to the mother have to do with two things: first, the tendency to live in a dual world, to divide the world into that which is strongly good and strongly bad, the failure to grow into a more mature sense of the relatedness of what is experienced as good and what is experienced as bad, of ambiguity as being normal. So the notion of extreme evil as opposed to extreme good, the splitting that we do, not only in terms of the personality, but also of nature as opposed to man, seems then to grow right out of that failure of connectedness.

The second kind of psychopathic behaviour related to this failure of bonding is the seeming necessity to control my immediate environment. The feeling that unless I control my body, it's going to go wrong. We project this kind of thing into our adult lives in which we try to control our bowels, our hormones, our emotions. That extends very easily to the natural world. We assume that nature gone wild is chaotic unless we control it. The river overrunning its banks is out of control. What grows out of this infantile fear of loss of control projects itself into our adult lives in different ways, and creates philosophies which support duality and control.

CAYLEY   It's clear that in so many ways what's going on in our world is the search for a new nature philosophy. You've certainly been part of that. Is this emerging ecological philosophy something that can come to terms with the world as it is and help to change it?

SHEPARD   You now come to the inevitable. We've talked about the problem, now what do we do? It's the question that my students come to in the first day of the course which I teach. I follow Ivan Illych on this question. He says, and I commit myself to the same view, 'I can't do everything.' It's all I can possibly do to get some hold on what might be part of the problem. Somebody else is going to have to deal with the question of solutions, of the machinery for making changes, and for how it's going to be done. Of course that is not a popular reply, and it doesn't make my students happy, but I think that I've only begun to be able to play a small role in understanding what the question is.

CAYLEY   I think that's a wonderful reply, because I think the language of problems and solutions is not the language one would want to apply in searching for the way of life that's appropriate for us.

SHEPARD   The language of solutions may be part of the problem.

SUGGESTED READINGS RELATING TO THIS INTERVIEW:

Murray Bookchin, *Toward an Ecological Society*
(Montreal: Black Rose Books, 1980).

Neil Evernden, *The Natural Alien*
(Toronto: University of Toronto Press, 1985).

John Livingston, *The Fallacy of Wildlife Conservation*
(Toronto: McClelland & Stewart, 1981).

Paul Shepard, *Nature and Madness* (Sierra Books, 1983).

Allen Dregson, ed., 'Voices from the Canadian Ecophilosophy Network,'
The Trumpeter (Victoria, B.C.: Lightstar)

JULIA BLUSHAK

RICK/SIMON

THE SWAN AND LEDA

I HAVE A LOT OF RESPECT for William Butler Yeats, but I've got to tell you his famous poem 'Leda and the Swan' isn't accurate. The alleged rape of Leda didn't happen the way he described it. It was a very different kind of event. Swans do not rape. They don't have to. And only those who have gazed into the eyes of a swan will truly understand why.

Relax. I'm not writing this from jail. I haven't had sex with a swan. But I have met one, and I have looked into its eyes. In quite a non-mystical way, I have communed with the swan, and it has given me an insight into the real story of Leda and Zeus and all the history that followed from that encounter.

'Take me home with you,' the swan whispered.

It didn't say why it wanted me to take it home. There was a delicious moment in which our eyes were locked.

'I don't even know if you're male or female,' I said without thinking.

'Who cares?' said the swan.

'I can't take you home,' I said, tearing my gaze from the swans and trying to sound more firm than I felt. 'I'm a human being, and you're a swan. You don't belong in my world.'

I thought about my two cats, one of which is inordinately fond of birds. Recently it coldcocked an unsuspecting seagull that happened to land in its small but extremely immediate sphere of attention. The cat pounced on it, knocked it senseless, and was proudly dragging its very large acquisition into the house through an open window when the gull regained consciousness. The ensuing melee left the place in a shambles. I also have a part-labrador pup who shows a certain genetically based interest in chasing birds of any kind. My

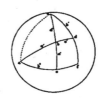

house is no place for a sweet-eyed bird.

'I love you,' the swan cooed, interrupting my unspoken run of excuses.

'Aw, come on,' I chided. 'You love everybody. I can see it in your eyes. And if it makes you feel better, I like you too. A lot. But I can't take you home with me.'

'How about something to eat, then,' the swan countered reproachfully. I rummaged through my pockets, instantly feeling guilty. 'I brought a bag of birdseed,' I said apologetically, 'but my kids fed it to the ducks. All I've got now is some potato chips.'

The swan cocked its head without taking its eyes off me. 'What flavour are they?' it cooed, shuffling a little closer to the fence.

'Taco.'

'Shit. I despise taco flavoured chips. They upset my stomach. I only like the plain ones.'

'I'm sorry,' I mumbled. 'They tasted fine to me.'

The swan looked away, as if unable to bear the disappointment. Then it turned back to me.

'Will you come back next week?' it asked, looking straight into my eyes once again. 'Please?'

I felt like a chicken trying to avoid the hypnotic gaze of a cobra. Well, no, it wasn't quite that bad. I *tried* to feel like I was being manipulated. No luck.

I glanced over at my two sons. They were staring at me suspiciously. Their father was having a conversation with a large bird, which was, after all, something they had not encountered on television except maybe on *Sesame Street*. And they know that the bird on that program is really only a man dressed up to look something like a bird. In their eyes, my behavior was inappropriate, and maybe weird. I felt a small swirl of resentment toward them, not so much because they disapproved of the swan and me, but because they'd wasted the entire bag of birdseed getting some

 stupid ducks to follow them around like they were the Pied Pipers. And now, the little egomaniacs were deciding that I was crazy.

'Bring me some sardines,' the swan whispered, bending its neck and poking its soft head through the wire fence into my hand. 'King

Oscar. They're so much better than the cheaper brands.'

'You do this to lots of people,' I said to the swan. 'Don't you?'

'No,' the swan answered quietly. There was a hint of irony in its voice. 'You're the very first.'

I haven't gone back. I have a complicated life as it is, and I know that if I were to go back I might do anything the swan asked, and that in a very short time my life would be ruined, cats, dogs, kids and all. And anyway, literature is full of those kinds of stories, even if life doesn't seem to be anymore.

Lets go back to Mr. Yeats. Some parts of his poem are correct. He was correct in thinking that swans are capable of having sexual intercourse with human beings. Most birds can't, including eagles, ravens, condors and vultures. Ostriches can, but it doesn't seem to happen very often. Only a select few birds have the right equipment, and swans are atop the list. The rest of the birds on the planet make do with an all-purpose cloaca, and when they mate, it is aerial, instantaneous, a brief bum-bump in the bright air. I've known a few people—mostly women, actually—who complain about their men on roughly the same terms, but for most of us, sexual experience is a little more complicated, and, er, deeper and longer.

Second, I can't see any reason to doubt that Zeus did conceive a passion of sorts for the beautiful Leda, but there is reason to question the nature of that passion as depicted by Yeats and by some of the old myths. In the cosmology of the Greeks, the gods, unlike human beings, rarely had only one thing in mind, and Zeus, who was the chief god, always had an ulterior motive— usually an educative one.

The Greeks (who after all invented Zeus) needed to put an end to the powerful city of Troy because it sat directly in the path of all the best trade routes to Asia Minor. Leda was the medium and the opportunity for producing precisely the right mix of passions and abilities that would lead to Troy's destruction. So, into the body of the swan Zeus leaped, meta- phorically speaking. An indeterminate time later, Leda, presumably also metaphorically, is said to have laid one or two or four eggs, de- pending on whose version of the story you ac- cept as the correct one.

We could reduce the story to boring discussion of the nature of metaphor or of local politics if we pursue this line of explanation much further. And we'd be missing the point—and the fun. So let's get back to Yeats and his telling of the tale. It is in his depiction of the coupling of god and woman that Mr. Yeats loses control of his materials. We can accept, for the sake of the tale, that Zeus conceived a divine passion for Leda. No problem. But the other side of the Yeats story is all wrong.

I figure that Leda must have fallen for a swan, possibly in much the same way I fell for mine. For months, every weekend, she went to the bird sanctuary just outside Sparta with the equivalent of the King Oscar sardines my swan asked me for. Zeus must have spotted her at the bird sanctuary—he was a well-known bird-watcher and merely hopped inside her chosen swan to take advanrage of the attraction that was already in full bloom.

Their union couldn't have been a brutal one. There was almost certainly a tentativeness in it, a sweetness, soft billings and cooings. Thighs and feathers stroked alike. Probably there was a quiet discussion of the anatomical awkwardnesses, and during and after their lovemaking, a great deal of tenderness. And if, at the moment of orgasm the swan lifted his great wings, spread them across Leda's thighs and let loose a cry of ecstasy, well, what of it? Leda was probably vocalizing at the same time. I'm willing to bet big bucks that most people have heard or made noises—screams, groans and grunts—of less aesthetically pleasing quality, and a few (not me, of course) have made invocations to a deity. Maybe it was an invocation from Leda that gave the locals the idea that she was getting it on with an important god.

Yeats raises the question of whether or not, in the midst of her ecstasy, Leda understood the divine intentions within her swan. Translated, he was asking if she saw how the sensible but quite business-like political intelligence of Greece was going to destroy the threat of Troy, and how, having done so, it would deal with the megalomania of its victorious forces.

On a slightly different track, it is revealing that the Greeks have argued bitterly over every aspect of this story except the reality and purpose of Leda coupling with the swan. Some, for instance, said that only Helen of Troy was born of the union, and that the other three children born at the same time were merely mortal and relatively unfated. Others argued for different combinations of mortality and divinity, egg or live birth.

None of them seemed to have thought it unusual that Leda had sexual intercourse that same night with her husband Tyndareus, and no one mentioned that in her supposedly bruised and violated condition, the husband noted nothing untoward about her appearance and demeanor. And, notwithstanding the renowned sensitivity of modern Greek males, you should be convinced by that fact alone that no act of violence took place with the swan.

One of the other offspring of that steamy afternoon tryst in ancient Greece, became, in her way, as famous as Helen. This was Helen's sister, Clytemnestra. She and Helen married brothers, and it was Clytemnestra who married the more powerful of the two. She married Agamemnon, who was the High King of all the Mycenaean tribes, and was the commander of the Greek force that attacked Troy after Paris kidnapped Helen. Clytemnestra believed that her husband sacrificed one of their daughters in order to get the Greek fleet to Ilium. And when, ten years later, Agamemnon returned in overweening triumph, and with a dozen or so docile Trojan concubines in his luggage, his wife and her lover murdered him before he had time to sit down in his own living room. This set off another series of events, the Oresteia, and that set off another, and so on and so forth, until you find yourself wondering why you don't get along easily with your family, and I find myself wondering how long it would take to nip on out to the bird refuge.

STORIES LIKE THAT sort of make life sound reasonable and grand and connected, don't they? The Greek message is always the same: Life resonates, and we are inevitably, unalterably part of those resonances if we look and listen carefully enough.

One of the things I like about myth is that it just isn't a commercial medium. When we talk in mythic terms, no matter what we do, no matter the numbers of Hostess Twinkies that sulk, half digested, in our intestines, we are within a continuum of events that links us in a common narrative, a story which is at once personal and common to all. Sure, the action these days is often fouled by commercials, and most of us fall asleep in the parts where the story doesn't seem to be about us, but that's because we've been conned into thinking the complexities of existence are voluntary; that in a democracy, participation is optional.

You're not sure what I'm talking about? Well, as I write this, there is a woman walking along the street toward the cafe I'm sitting in. She is a slight woman, stoop-shouldered, perhaps thirty years old. She walks with the staggering gait of someonewho is recurrently and chronically afraid, and thus attempts to see in all dark directions at once. Both her eyes are blackened from some sort of beating. But unaccountably she is grinning, almost idiotically. Perhaps she is ironically chiding herself for having walked into a door. Perhaps she is on her way to a centre for battered women. On the bright side, perhaps she has just landed a hatchet in the forehead of her slopeheaded husband, or she's seen her favorite heroine on the afternoon television soap operas similarly dispatch a tormentor. More depressingly, perhaps she's merely bombed on the tranquillizers her family doctor has given her in order to help her adjust to her domestic difficulties. And perhaps, she has just made love with a swan. Perhaps, perhaps; the possibilities are almost infinite. And all of them are connected.

This isn't *quite* the way the Greeks would have seen it, nor is it the world according to W.B. Yeats. Writing more than a half-century ago, Yeats still believed that a reasonable and grand and connected order was at the heart of human existence—a cosmology, to use the vernacular. For him, Zeus was the personification of all that, a benign magnificence that drew some of the animal violence out of the planet by means of a grand scheme to defuse brute chaos and then to give it structure. All else that was good, for Yeats, followed from that impulse toward order.

The Greeks didn't try to create so absolute an order by their  speculation and tales. Instead, they observed, they talked, and they cherished the multiplicity and apparent confusion of the world without pushing it all the way to the kind of abstract order Yeats craved. Nor did they seek mercy from its whirling pinions; they saw its goodness in the necessity of constantly rebuilding and retooling the stories by which they understood the infinite complexity we are in.

AND WHAT IS IT that we do, we who live without cosmology, and are deluged with lifestyle fictions that say nothing of life's complexity? Let me tell you a tale of the world we inhabit:

Several years ago, in the main part of the city I live in, swans began to die under mysterious circumstances. The autopsies carried out at the local zoo soon uncovered a single cause for the deaths. The swans had died because their necks had been broken. The newspaper and television stories about the swans, accompanied always by gruesome film and photographs of the mutilated birds, received a great deal of publicity, and soon a heated public debate was taking place. What was killing the swans? What or who was the villain? A pack of marauding dogs was identified as the most likely culprit, and the SPCA and the Parks Board argued over which agency had the responsibility for capturing the dogs. While this went on, several more swans were killed. When no dogs were found, it was suggested that raccoons were responsible. Now the wildlife branch joined the struggle to elude responsibility for stopping the slaughter. And more swans died.

One evening late in the summer, a pair of lovers happened to be couched in the park near the spot where the swans congregated for the night. From their accidental and initially blissful vantage point amidst the park's lush foliage, they saw a young man approach the water's edge. The man began to speak in a soft voice to a flock of swans, throwing them scraps of bread as he spoke. Then, as they watched, spellbound as it were, the man removed his clothing, brushed back his short blond hair, and waded carefully into the water. He continued to talk to the swans in the same calm tones, and soon one bird drew close to him. He reached out his hand to stroke the sleek neck of the bird, as one might stroke a lover, and the swan bent its head to accept thc caress. Then the man strangled the swan.

The couple instantly realized who the wader was, and had the presence of mind to steal his clothing Then they ran through the park with it, half-clothed themselves, and flagged down a policeman in a patrol car. After a few minutes of questioning, the policeman accepted their story, and several more patrol cars were summoned. The swan-killer was taken into custody, pushed into the back of one of the patrol cars to the flashing pops and quiet whinings of the media cameras, which appeared as they always do, seconds after the arrest was made.

The police went through the normal scene-of-the-crime procedures. The lovers were asked several difficult questions about what they were doing in the park, and photographs were taken of the dead swan, which still floated, half-submerged, in the lagoon. The media took their own photographs of the swan, pressing close to and into the water in order to gain the most sensational possible angle. And indeed, the newspaper photograph that appeared the next day revealed small particles of a glutinous white substance floating in the water around the body of the swan.

The suspect openly, even proudly, admitted to killing the other swans. He offered no explanation for why he'd killed them, and nobody in the press or media seemed to think that an explanation was required. Crazy people are good news. Why people go crazy isn't. The man was charged with an awkward and obscure summary offense; pleaded guilty and was convicted, and quickly committed for psychiatric observation. After three months, he was released, and is presumably somewhere on the streets right now.

ISN'T THAT A DREADFUL ANECDOTE? You may be asking yourself why I related it. It's really awful, filled with gratuitous violence, sexual perversion and moral turpitude, right? Did you notice that it also has highly coherent cinematographic sets, some suspense, a little terror, some careful exposure of skin, and a cynical depiction of the ineptness of our public agencies? It's just like a television drama, if you think about it. Right now, you're probably about to toss this onto the coffee table and head out to the kitchen for a snack. Diet Pepsi? Hostess Twinkies? How's your underarm deodorant holding up?

Sorry about not having a nice ending, but it's the world we live in that prevents that. We have all the information and all the sensation, but none of the stories we hear quite add up. They just pile up, a different kind of assault altogether. ◉

EVERY PROSPECT
PLEASES

*Our gardener-in-residence offers
some tips on tending the in-house garden*

QUESTION My husband and I have a house full of plants and animals and sometimes they don't get along very well. Do you have any suggestions for keeping our household happy?

GARDENESQUE Plants and pets do not always live as harmoniously together as one might wish. Dogs are clumsy, and cats, being natural detectives, have to check out every blooming thing. There are ways to lessen the damage: chili powder, white or cayenne pepper, or split, dried hot peppers pressed into the houseplant's soil, are effective deterrents. Hot mustard works well too, and can be applied to the plant's lower leaves—but it does look revolting! Avoid placing a new houseplant anywhere your pet has staked a prior claim, such as the sunny window where Fido has taken his afternoon snooze since time immemorial.

Some plants are actually hazardous to pets and young children. These include holly—particularly the berries—Jerusalem cherry, bittersweet, and spindle berry; mistletoe means death.

B. KLUNDER

QUESTION I am one of those people who has terrible luck with houseplants. They look fine when I bring them into the house, but in two weeks they're goners. What can I do?

GARDENESQUE There are

many reasons why your plants might be biting the dust. Here are a few tips that helped.

One fact has to be faced—sooner or later all houseplants become dinner to hungry bugs. In dire circumstances I prefer a swift death rather than weeks of washing, soaping, rinsing, dabbing, isolating, and spraying—hard on the plants and hell on the owner. For about twelve dollars, Richter's in Goodwood, Ontario (tel.: 416-640-6677 for charge-card orders) will dispatch a packet of cunning Yellow Sticky Strips.* These consist of several yellow 13 cm x 10 cm (5" x 4") cards impreganted with a sweetish, sticky substance irresistible to insects. Flying, fluttering, hopping, skittering, and crawling, they rush to the strips where they stick fast.

Six 30-cm (12") metal skewers are provided in each packet. Each skewer has a double loop at one end into which, with some difficulty, the strips are inserted. Wear rubber gloves and have a bottle of rubbing alcohol or paint thinner at hand. One strip serves 45 cm (18") of plant arrangement, and will last for two or three months.

Potted indoor plants abhor the following: indoor stuffy heat, sudden or continual draughts, being constantly moved from one location to another, dry air, over-watering, sunstroke, over-fertilizing, isolation from other plants, foliage touching icy window panes, too much fingering, and investigation by curious cats.

Houseplants benefit if grouped together as the humidity is greater. This also makes it easier to clear up their debris—falling leaves and the like. Place them on a large, stable surface on waterproof trays covered with a layer of pebbles to a depth of 5 cm (2"). Set the pots on upturned saucers and keep the pebbles constantly moist. More plants die from over-watering than from drought. During the winter when light levels are low, plants need less water. The further away a plant is from a direct light source,

---

* There are nine yellow strips in each packet. They are smeared with tanglewood, the unctuous preparation that one normally paints on trees to prevent moths from laying eggs. Tanglewood is made of natural resins and substances to keep the preparation from drying out. Richter's sells these strips for $10.15, plus a $2 handling charge for an order of one packet only.

Since this was written, "Yellow Sticky Strips" are available at most nurseries and plant stores. They come in two sizes with easier-to-use plastic holders.

HERE IS MY LIST of foolproof and reasonably attractive houseplants. Add to it all forced bulbs as they come into bloom.

Low light	Medium light	High light
Aspidistra	African violet	Amaryllis
Boston fern	Aralia	Bay
Chinese evergreen	Asparagus fern	Browallia
Dieffenbachia	Begonia	Cacti
Spathiphyllum	Bromeliads	Citrus (esp. grapefruit)
Swedish ivy	Clivia	Coleus
(hanging)	Coral berry	Flowering maple
Creeping fig	False aralia	Geranium
Moneywort	Ficus benjamina	German ivy
Rosary vine	Fuchsia	Impatiens (winter
Spider plant	Fatshedra lizei	only—remove to
	Philodendron	shade in spring and
	(hanging)	summer)
	Cissus	Myrtle
	(a.k.a.'grape ivy')	Rosemary
	Velvet plant	
	Wandering jew	

the less water it needs. Many plants spend the winter in a semi-dormant condition, storing their energy, and resting before the spring. Ideal indoor plant temperatures are 18-22°C (64-72°F) by day, and 14-18°C (57-64°F) by night.

Assess the amount of light available before choosing indoor plants. High light is 4-5 hours of direct sun per day. Medium light is 2-4 hours of direct sun per day plus lots of bright light at other times. Low light is 1-3 hours of direct sun per day, and lots of bright light at other times (or no direct sunlight, but with bright light from windows facing north or east). Plants will not grow in unlit interior gloom, although they may survive—just.

House plants from plant specialists usually arrive with growing instructions. Supermarkets and dime stores are less likely to provide the novice with pertinent information.

Mist the air around plants three times a week with tepid water. When watering, draw the water the night before to allow the chemicals to settle. Avoid splashing water onto each plant's leaves—plants hate wet leaves. ◉

HONOUR THY INGREDIENTS

Cooking Philosophies of Michael Stadtlander & Chris Klugman

MICHAEL STADTLANDER was born in Lubeck, West Germany, in 1957, and raised on a farm there. While in Lucerne, Switzerland, he met Jamie Kennedy, a young Canadian chef, and together they caused a sensation in Toronto opening Scaramouche restaurant. Michael has won national acclaim for his innovative Canadian cuisine, which draws on the bounty of the forests, waters, and markets of Ontario and the Pacific Northwest.

CHRIS KLUGMAN gave up his studies in engineering in 1980 to cook professionally, beginning in the Kingston, Ontario, vegetarian restaurant, Scarecrow. Klugman found a kindred spirit in Michael Stadtlander, sharing a love for nature, wild foods, and the imaginative use of fresh ingredients.

JWC   What is the ideal restaurant for you?

KLUGMAN   I'm tempted to say the ideal setup would be a two-person restaurant—one person in front to serve people in a comfortable way and the other in the kitchen preparing the meals. The problem is that it is unfair to the many people who could be contributing to the restaurant and at the same time learning how to cook. One chef (i.e., just me) is tempting but unfair. If we want food to be a significant part of our culture and if we don't want cooking to become a lost art, it is necessary to pass on that awareness and the only way to do that is by teaching in restaurants.

JWC   What is your opinion of wild foods?

KLUGMAN   Wild foods should be a central part of Canadian

ILLUSTRATIONS BY BARBARA KLUNDER

cooking. First of all because we have them. Canada is unique in that we still have resources whereas so many European countries have to go elsewhere—to Canada, for instance—to find them. But the fact is we don't use them, we don't take advantage of the land—or at least we don't use it properly. Also, it's a question of priorities. The wild foods are there but to a great extent they're unknown. Instead we buy crayfish from Louisiana.

STADTLANDER I've heard that part of Russian caviar is Canadian, and that chanterelles are being picked up here by German companies, put in cans, and shipped to Germany; they come back as German chanterelles from the Bavarian forests! We've got to come out of this naive stage and become masters of our own industry.

KLUGMAN Michael was telling me about pine mushrooms from the west coast. I've never seen them but it seems that they're being sold to Japan. So someone recognizes our resources.

JWC Can you give us an example of how you are practicing an indigenous cuisine?

STADTLANDER We're using some foods that might represent a kind of Canadian cuisine. For instance, we're using chicken mushrooms, which no one has ever heard of, but they're there. And then we're concerned with cooking them properly. We're doing it in such a way that the ingredients can be appreciated in and for themselves. In other words, you don't cook them in a pot with other vegetables, with California vegetables. My philosophy has always been that food should be presented as an extension of where it's grown.

JWC In 1987 you two formed a catering partnership that culminated in the dinner 'Toronto/Northwest.' Tell us something about that.

KLUGMAN The main idea of the partnership was to highlight Canadian cooking. Michael has been out west learning to cook what's available there, and I've been here, using local Toronto food—the food that's available in this city's markets. What we were doing then was bringing together two distinctly different regions of Canada.

STADTLANDER Before I came to Scaramouche (in Toronto), I was working in a style of French *nouvelle cuisine*. But we were using German products, products that were distinctive of specific regions of Germany, such as Gutenberg. But in doing that kind of thing I was trying to transfer German ideas of cooking to Canada. It didn't work.

JWC Why didn't it work?

STADTLANDER It's a totally different mentality here, partly because the restaurant scene in Canada in the late seventies was just beginning to change. Now it is much more European, and less commercial, I think. So far as I can tell the restaurant business in Canada has in the past tended to be just that—a business, a way of making money. It used to be hard to find a waiter who was proud of his job. But that's changing. Now it's popular to go to cafés and restaurants where the chef is regarded as an artist.

JWC You mentioned that when you first came here from Europe you were cooking in the style of French nouvelle cuisine. Can you define what you mean by that term?

STADTLANDER It's an evolution from classical cuisine. It is different in many ways from the classical, but I think the greatest difference has to do with the freedom of the chef. He or she is not tied down by established rules of cooking. It's like modern art as opposed to classical art. The chef is more than an interpreter, playing the same piece over and over again in only slightly different ways. It's more spontaneous and I think more creative. There's an element of freshness or originality in it that also means that the person who comes to the restaurant is not going to be bored with the same thing every time. Still, I don't want to make it appear that nouvelle cuisine has no relation to classical traditions in cooking. It's part of an evolution. Also, I don't really like to say that I do 'nouvelle cuisine', because that in itself is a limitation if it's taken to represent a specific approach governed by specific rules.

KLUGMAN The concept that Fernand Point—the inventor of *nouvelle cuisine*—first tried to get across was that you put the sauce under the meat rather than on top of it. The fundamental idea is to highlight the ingredients, the quality and freshness of the ingredients rather than trying to mask them and make them appear like they're something else. You try instead to bring out what is intrinsically good in each particular ingredient. That's a very modern notion of cooking.

JWC   When you two were at Stadtlander's—a restaurant, I assume, where you had it the way you wanted it—how were things different than when you were working in other restaurants?

STADTLANDER   We had the freedom to do what we wanted. We limited the menu to a few things and changed frequently. Part of this was to make the customers part of the process. They could see what we were up to by looking at the menu. That freedom would be impossible if you had a menu that included too many things. There was purpose to the way we did things and I think that that produced a kind of team spirit in the restaurant. We worked together. We'd go to the market to get fresh produce.

JWC   Stadtlander's was not a financial success, closing in the summer of 1985. Has this discouraged you from owning another restaurant?

STADTLANDER   For me the ideal would be represented by a restaurant that could serve as a sort of connecting point for new possibilities. I'd set up a schedule of visits every year during which new cooking ideas could be introduced. I'm thinking of things such as the Haida Indian method of steaming clams in cedar boxes. Things like that. But it could also be a way of introducing new products such as salmonberries and loganberries—shipping them directly from the farm in Vancouver Island to Toronto.

There's another side to this. The Haida Indian thing, for instance, might suggest to some that there's more to Canada than chopping down trees and wiping out whole cultures.   ◉

THE OWLS

We undress at the edge of the dark woodlot
and slip under the skin of the lake.
On the bottom of the pond
there is a dusky village the
dream of a child sleeping
in the back seat of a car.

Tonight even the owls
are dreaming on the wing,
soundless flickering stains in
the dark sanctum of night's night.
They break their predatory silence
with the eerie spectral address
of dream hunters.
The terrible beaks and claws of night.

All things here writhe, twist somehow as
ciphers in the dream's earthen logic.
Here at the eve of self where
we falter before each other's divinity
locked into our skin, distant
strangely & cruelly numb to the other.

Yet now, embracing underwater
our bodies come unlocked and
with the flesh of angels
we gush upwards, rising
from the night lake
in a storm of music. And there
in the absolute theatre of night
we fuse, recover
the lost disorder of the stars.

Depth Sounding, Lake Windermere

Suspended
    on the still surface of the night lake
we paddle silently towards the shore.
Its mysterious presence a kind of muteness, an assertion
equivocal to our liquid passage.
On the beach
a stand of birch
becomes a grove of fossil lightning
in the blinding silence
of a full summer moon.

Our paddles conspire purchase
in an invisible plane
glistening, imageless.
Each stroke leaving
two whirlpools,
    whispering vortexes which zipper up
a single vocable.
Utterance from
the depths of the lake.

NATURAL SELECTION

'ANYTHING YOU CAN THINK OF YOU CAN FIND.'
Barbara McClintock, geneticist, Nobel Laureate.

WE LIVE ON A PLANET where a species of animal becomes extinct every month. The power of nature is in its multiplicity, its power of adaptation and reproduction. Animals, with their long history of survival, will continue to adapt to their environment as they have in the past. As man changes the biosphere, non-human animals do not die away. They find new, more efficient ways to live with human populations in urban environments.

We study animal populations by isolating individuals of a species in our zoos, natural history museums, and television nature programs. In *Natural Selection*, I have attempted to dream about animals from the inside, and to replenish our world from the imagination.

PRINT GRUB (*Visus litteratum*)
The North American print grub is a well-known pest infecting libraries and bookstores. This tiny grub has a transparent, lens-like body that distorts the print below it and gives the impression of a typographical error or misprint.*

The print grub lives on book pages and licks the ink up off the page, slowly erasing whole lines of type as it feeds. The grub digests the gum arabic or glue content of the ink and defecates the pigment residue, leaving behind an unsightly smudge.

EXAMPLE OF INFECTED TEXT

The print grub has become a significant

pest in large North American libraries, reducing entire books to defecatory blobs. In recent years, researchers in the Saskatchewan Bibliographic Centre have discovered marked tendencies in the print grub's habits. For instance, statistics show a consistent predilection for glossy magazines. No infestation has been found in the works of William Shakespeare, Marcel Proust, Henrik Ibsen or Mervyn Peake, although volumes on nearby stacks were considerably infested. It may be going too far to suggest that print grubs are executing a type of literary criticism; yet, the facts are undeniable.

* Typographical errors in this publication may be attributable to print grubs. Please check carefully.

SENOFLEX (*Fungii anthropodis*)

The senoflex is the first human-created animal, developed in Sweden from a 'mutant fungus that replicates plant and animal tissue. Swedish scientists first discovered this fungus attached to trees, perfectly mimicking the host's bark. Laboratory tests showed that it could reproduce any living tissue. The breakthrough occurred when it was grafted onto a laboratory hamster; it absorbed the DNA pattern of the surrounding animal tissue and duplicated it.

After this discovery, human DNA was implanted in a cultured senoflex, and the senoflex perfectly repro-

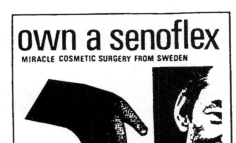

own a senoflex

MIRACLE COSMETIC SURGERY FROM SWEDEN

senoflex replacement of 2ⁿᵈ finger · a replaced ear

Through the miracle of modern science a completely safe, hygenic and non-detectable artificial limb is now available— the miraculous Senoflex. Requiring no special fit or maitenance the Senoflex is generated from your own DNA makeup: it is your part as nature had intended.

Developed in Sweden thousands have benefited from Senoflex implants in Europe, where they have proved natural looking, practical and very **write today THE SENOFLEX ASSOCIATION**

safe. The Senoflex, once installed, is never removed or altered, it is your artifical part for life. The only limitation is that the Senoflex is an artifical limb and has no powers of movement.

The Senoflex, because it is grown from your own body genes, is a completely realistic aid. See your local Senoflex distributing asgent and get all the information on this extraordinary and inexpensive medical miracle today!

duced the coded human part. Thus, missing or disfigured human parts can be replaced using host-generated genes; new ears or fingers can be grown from a person's own genetic code. As real as it looks, however, it must be remembered that the senoflex is not human tissue but an animal parasite. If, for example, someone is missing an ear, the senoflex is grafted onto the side of the head and implanted with a gene. It then grows to duplicate the lost ear. The senoflex cannot function with the human body because it is not linked to the nervous system (i.e., a senoflex finger cannot move). Thus, active human parts such as internal organs cannot be replaced with passive senoflex parasites.

The senoflex lives off the host's body, having no metabolic functions itself. It lives on the fluids of the host, and maintains only a single animal function: reproduction. Left unchecked, these spores would begin growing new senoflex all over the body (in this case in the form of the missing ear). This rather grotesque and fatal result is avoided in humans by the use of a special blood-cleansing drug that kills the senoflex spores without harming the parent senoflex or its human host. With proper grafting and care, the senoflex is a blessing to the many recipients in need of cosmetic parts.

LIGHTSWITCH BEETLE (*Lampadyria volticum*)

Lampadyria volticum is found in upper-class apartment buildings on the east coast of the United States, especially in New York City. This member of the family *Coleoptera* has developed the extraordinary camouflage of an Art Deco lightswitch, and lives exclusively in Art Deco buildings. Sensitive to light, it freezes on the wall when the lights are turned on in a room, retracting its legs and antennae and simulating a wall switch. The beetle feeds in darkness, eating peeling wallpaper or framed prints.

LIVE SPECIMEN

Lampadyria has four wings. The first pair are greatly thickened, forming wingcovers, or elytra, beneath which the membranous hind wings are folded at rest. The metamorphosis of this beetle is complete.

male

The body is shiny and black. The hind tarsi (legs) have four joints, the middle tarsi five joints. The head is concealed underneath the carapace. The elaborate prothorax margins of the elytra and the prothorax itself are greatly expanded, forming a circular outline. The great horn on the back of the Lightswitch Beetle is both for camouflage and defence.

HOLY CROSS FROG (*Amphibia religiosa*)

This mythical animal was at the foot of Christ's cross when he was crucified, a drop of holy blood scarring a cross on its back. Much prized by Russian saints, these frogs were kept in small boxes to amaze the common people. Pope Innocent XIII had a robe made of the skins of eighty-five of these frogs, to be worn on special occasions.

BUTT ROACH (*Roachus cindricus*)

The butt roach is the only life form known to survive on a completely carbon diet. It lives in ashtrays, feeding on carbon slag and nicotine residues. It is also one of the few insects that demonstrably suffers from nervous system disorders and cancer. *Roachus* is an ephemera, with an average life span of only eighteen hours. The insects lay their eggs in the filters of cigarette butts, which hatch as nymphs. The first of the hatching nymphs eats the other eggs and then transforms within the larval skin. It feeds on carbon and tar, developing legs that protrude from the butt and enable it to move about in the manner of a hermit crab, laying eggs. The body remains soft inside the fibrous cocoon of the filter.

Since their discovery in 1981, these insects have become central to cancer research. They provide ideal subjects for studying all types of degenerative cancers and nervous disorders. Their

Adult lays eggs in a discarded butt.   Eggs germinate   The first nymph to hatch eats other eggs   Pupal stage   Imago maintains butt as a portable camouflage

METAMORPHOSIS OF 'ROACHUS CINDRICUS'

only drawback is their very short lifespan, which rules out long-term observation. Recordings of *Roachus* mating calls, when slowed and amplified, sound distinctly like a low, whooping cough.

HOMING RAT (*Ratus problematicus*)

Ratus represents the only known example of a written language generated by an animal. Between 1951 and 1954, the Detroit Institute of Behavioral Psychology (DIBP) did research in artificially induced hysteria. Experiments involved running rats through mazes that were continuously changed during learning. After months of running and learning mazes that consistently denied food rewards, the rats began rolling around, lacerating their stomachs with their teeth. Researchers originally concluded that this behaviour was an hysterical response to intolerable frustration.

During a fire that broke out on April 14, 1954, many of these rats escaped, fleeing into the Detroit sewer system. From there they spread to other urban centres. These rats, living in chaotic, man-made cities, continued their habit of lacerating their stomachs, and developed the ability to formulate marks that helped them to orient themselves in their territory. The small wounds turned into permanent pictographic scars related directly to certain features in the environment: burrow hole, street corner, etc. If the rat became disoriented, it felt its stomach with its paws; the scars acted as a kind of braille map to re-orient the rat on its forages. Experts now agree that this behaviour evolved in the DIBP laboratories, where the rats lacerated themselves, not out of frustration, but out of an impulse to establish some form of permanent record of the constantly changing mazes that they were forced to run. In the wild, the rats have developed a standardized 'vocabulary' of fifteen environmental features represented by graphic scars.

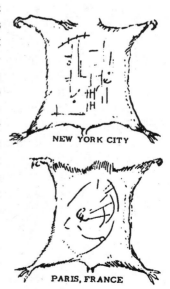

NEW YORK CITY

PARIS, FRANCE

DEATH FISH (*Electrophorus mortuous scaber*)

To live in an environment fatal to any other Teleosts (boney fishes) is the achievement of *Electrophorus mortuous scaber*, the death fish. Adapted to survive in highly polluted ponds and lakes, this fish digests mercury and secretes it to its outer skin layers, giving it a robotic, metallic appearance.

The more mercury-polluted the pond, the more brilliantly silvered the death fish. Its electrical organs are located in the  orbit, just behind the eyes. The eyes are at the side of the head, and can be protruded at will like those of the plaice. The mechanism for this is a kind of hydraulic device in the form of a small sac filled with fluid at the posterior ridge of the orbit. It can be compressed so as to drive the fluid into another sac behind the eyeball, thus pushing the eyeball outward. Behind the eyes are two large oval plates, and it has been established that the eye muscles, laced with heavy metal deposits, have evolved into electrical sources.

The death fish sees its prey and then delivers a shock, transmitted through the water. Although the fish is small, it can deliver a considerable charge; this is caused no doubt by the very high metal content of the fish's tissues. The death fish of Swartz Creek, Michigan, site of one of the most hazardous toxic waste dumps in the United States, can deliver a shock that can kill a child or cat. Toxic waste dumps in lakes near ChemDyne in Ohio, the Stringfellow acid pits in California, and Love Canal in New York State all have high concentrations of very dangerous schooling death fish, which are believed to have descended from innocent guppies used in water purity tests by the companies. Recent studies of the fish have revealed that they are slowly 'robotizing,' replacing organic tissues with metal deposits. Death fish are reported to have a curious habit of protruding their heads from the water and gazing at the stars at night. ◉

RETURN OF THE GODDESS

When God Was a Woman

A LONG, LONG TIME AGO, in the very beginnings of human life, in Europe, Asia, and Africa, people revered the mother of all life. Just as they'd been born from their own mothers, they envisioned a mother who had given birth to the cosmos and the very first people in the world. The Creator was the first mother.

Goddess worship, so widespread in ancient periods, was gradually suppressed and obliterated by later religions that worshipped male deities. This period of patriarchy began about 5000 years ago. As male gods took precedence over the ancient goddess and her female clergy, men assumed the right to make all the major decisions, because the male god had given them that right. What was left of the powerful images of a female god was diffused in the beliefs of classical Greece and Rome, where the goddess was fractured into many parts, each subservient to the male god Zeus. The father had replaced the mother as the ultimate deity.

The origin of civilization is generally associated with the development of written language. According to archaeological evidence examined by Merlin Stone in her book *When God Was a Woman*, writing was first developed in a temple of the Goddess in ancient Sumer.

MERLIN STONE This writing was found on tablets discovered in the deepest levels of the temple of the goddess Inanna, levels that are dated to about 3200 B.C. It seems most likely that this writing was developed by the priestesses of the goddess, priestesses known as the Naditu—the women who were in charge of temple records.

The Sumerian pictographs gradually evolved into a more abstract shorthand, a form of writing we know as cuneiform, which is composed of small wedge-shaped lines. These are the earliest-known origins of our own alphabet. From that time on, there is a continuous body of writing, and it is from that very early writing that we've learned of the prayers and rituals and legends of the ancient Goddess.

Just a few centuries later, writing appeared in other areas of the Near and Middle East, in places such as Egypt, Elam, Ebla, and India, and in each of these areas the tablets reveal a worship of the Goddess. Despite all this written evidence, many people of today still think of archaic Greece and the writings attributed to Homer as the beginnings of written history. Homer is dated to about the 8th century B.C.; this means that well over 2000 years of literature and written materials have been ignored in general education. From each of the cultures that long preceded Homer, there are wonderful stories, prayers of reverence, and accounts of historical events. Many of these stories and prayers tell us about the Great Goddess, the deity most deeply revered by the majority of people in ancient periods.

The worship of the Great Goddess was suppressed and nearly obliterated by later religions that were introduced by people known as Indo-Europeans, or Indo-Aryans, people who invaded the goddess-worshipping cultures, people who worshipped male gods, father gods. But despite these invasions and the suppression of the goddess religions, in certain areas worship of the Goddess survived well into the Christian period. In Acts 19 of the New Testament, we read of Paul encountering the worship of the goddess Diana, the ancient Artemis, at the temple of Ephesus in Turkey. And as late as the 5th century, the Christian emperor Justinian converted the temples of the goddess Isis into Christian churches. In the 7th century, Mohammed eradicated the worship of the goddess Alat, which simply means 'goddess' in Arabic. In India, goddess reverence continued underground among the indigenous Dravidians, eventually reemerging in the Purana books of Hinduism as the goddess Davi or Kali.

While I was researching the evidence of ancient goddess worship for *When God Was a Woman,* examining the excavation sites and goddess temples, and studying the multitude of statues and artifacts in museums from London to Beirut, one of the questions I kept asking was, 'How did the ancient worship of God in the image of mother, of woman, turn into the worship of God in the image of father, of man?' Theologians, those scholars whose field is the study of God and religion, often say that God really has no specific form or image, certainly  not one that we can know. But most people today imagine God as an elderly man, a kind of grandfather up in the heavens. And even those who claim God has no form still refer to God as 'He.'

As I traced the times of change from the worship of the Goddess to the worship of a supreme male god in each area, I began to notice a pattern emerging. The change inevitably began shortly after an invasion of each area by aggressive nomadic tribes from the north. Anatolia (modern-day Turkey) had been invaded by Indo-European Hittites. India had been invaded by Indo-European Aryans, Iran had been invaded by Indo-European Aryans. Greece and Crete had been invaded by Indo-European Mycenaeans. The pattern began to take form. The invading tribes were quite different people from the indigenous peoples of each area, those who had worshipped the Goddess for so many thousands of years. Each of the invading groups had come from the north, and each had used some form of Indo-European language, revealing their connection to each other. I could find no archaeologist or historian who discussed this general pattern of invasions by Indo-European groups. Each scholar had concentrated on one specific geographic area. Yet it was clear from reading all of them together that the Indo-European-speaking tribes, at times referred to as Indo-Aryans or simply the Aryan tribes, were people who had developed a patriarchal way of life, honouring men above women and worshipping male gods, imagining them to live high on mountaintops, usually on volcanoes.

The same Indo-European-speaking peoples then invaded all of Europe, which had also been populated by goddess-worshipping people, and eventually migrated as far west as Ireland. They left us the legacy of the origins of most European languages, just as they left Sanskrit, which is an Indo-European language, in India. And they also left us patriarchal forms of society and the image of the supreme deity as male.

Goddess worship had always been closely associated with nature, with the cycles of the seasons and with celebrations of planting and harvesting times. Goddess worship was so deeply linked to nature that scholars often call it a nature religion. The high god of the Indo-Europeans was more removed from nature. The aggressive nomadic people had not settled into a life of farming and agriculture, and the Indo-European images of God were as a warrior, aggressive and conquering, images that not only condoned the invasions and conquests of other lands and other people, but encouraged them.

After the conquests of goddess-worshipping lands by Indo-European tribes, various images of deity began to form. One was the idea of a pair of gods, a married couple in which the husband was seen as the much greater power, while the wife—that is, the demoted goddess—had little power or importance. In some areas, such as in India and Babylon, legends explained that the male god had murdered the goddess and appropriated all of her knowledge and powers. These legends of the cosmic murder often took the form of the warrior god killing a dragon, whose name just happened to be the name of the goddess in that area. Such legends are probably the origins of the later myths about St. George and the dragon and St. Patrick and the snakes.

The archaeological evidence shows that worship of the Great Goddess did not simply fade away, but was eradicated in a series of invasions and conquests by Indo-European tribes over several thousand years. In Europe, goddess worship survived among the country people. The word 'pagan' in Latin simply meant a country person, while 'heathen' simply means people of the heath, the rural countryside. Well into the 17th and 18th centuries on the mainland of Europe, and in the British Isles, goddess worship continued in a religion followed by the Celtic people, a religion known as Wicca.

Today, many women regard the image of the Goddess purely as metaphor, a symbol of women's reclamation of personal power and the right to determine the path of our own lives. For many others, the Goddess is the focal point of religious and spiritual feelings. One of these women is Starhawk, whose books *The Spiritual Dance* and *Dreaming the Dark* explain the religion of Wicca.

Starhawk, why do the words witch and witchcraft frighten so many people?

STARHAWK I think clearly the reason they frighten so many people is that we've had 500 years of propaganda saying that witches and witchcraft are evil and frightening, and you should be scared of them. That was instituted by both the Catholic and Protestant churches as part of their campaign to wipe out what was really a rival religion, the old religion of Western Europe from before Christianity. Witches and witchcraft have also become associated with the idea of women and women's power, and particularly with power that is outside the control of the authorities, that does not come through the accepted channels—actually, whether it comes through women or men. And so that again it was made to be seen as something terrible and frightening and evil and nasty.

But what the word really means, the root of the word *wic* is an Anglo-Saxon word that means to bend or shape, and witches were those who could bend or shape consciousness. In other words, they were shamans, they were priestesses, they were those who could go in and out of different states of consciousness and awareness. They meditated, they created rituals, celebrations. They were in a sense the priesthood, or priestesshood, of the people. And so *witch* also has that secondary meaning of 'wit' or 'wisdom.' They were wise women. They were the ones who knew the healing herbs, they knew what to do in case of sickness. Often witches were midwives. Every village had its own healer in it before there were established doctors.

MERLIN STONE How does the worship or reverence of the Goddess in Wicca differ from the worship of God in what we call patriarchal religions, the masculist religions?

STARHAWK Wicca is not a belief system so much, not a set of things you are supposed to believe on *faith*. Probably every witch would give you a different definition of who the Goddess is and what she means. But more, it's a set of things that you do that create a strong set of values. When we say the earth is sacred or nature is sacred, to me what that means is that we then value the earth in a different way, we value it for itself, not so much for what it can do for us or how we can exploit it. We say women's bodies are sacred; then we have to value our own bodies in a deeper way. The other way that the goddess religion differs, I think, is that it's much more active and participatory. We say every witch is a priestess—there's no laity. And we do rituals together that are alive and fun and involving, and involve very little if any sitting around, listening to someone talk to you.

MERLIN STONE Do you think of the Goddess as up in heaven, or transcendent, or do you view the Goddess as within yourself, within each woman?

STARHAWK To me, the Goddess is immanent. That means she is within the entire living world. Historically, there have been earth goddesses and sky goddesses. There have been goddesses in human form, in animal form, all of those things. It doesn't really mean that people believed in a big lady in the sky. What it meant was that they recognized the sky was one manifestation of a power, a spirit, a living connection that flows through all living things, as if the whole universe were really one living body and we were all cells, parts of that body.

MERLIN STONE One of the major fears that people seem to have about witchcraft is that it's evil, that there's no concern for ethics or morality.

STARHAWK It came again from the propaganda that witchcraft was the worship of the Christian devil, Satanism. Actually, witchcraft has nothing to do with Satanism. From a witch's perspective, Satanism is a Christian heresy, because in order to believe in Satanism, you have to believe in the whole Christian belief system, and we don't believe in Satan, let alone worship Satan. But that again was part of the propaganda used to try to discredit the old religion, to try to make people fear it. It was part of the excuse for the torture and the burning and the killing of hundreds of thousands of women and men between the 16th and the 18th centuries.

MERLIN STONE So the whole idea really arose from the church's suppression of the old religion.

STARHAWK Right. Witchcraft does have a very strong sense of ethics. Our ethics are connected again with respecting the sacredness in the earth and in all living beings. And the energy that we work with in ritual has a way of sort of keeping you straight. Be-

cause we have a saying that anything you say and anything you put out through ritual, through magic, through prayer returns on you three times over. It's like the Golden Rule amplified. So we believe that you cannot harm somebody without harming yourself in the process.

MERLIN STONE One of the most interesting ideas developing within women's spirituality is that of goddess, not as a form or a being, but as a process. Mary Daly (author of *Beyond God The Father*) writes that we should see the ultimate deity not as a noun, but as a verb. Z. Budapest says that the male god may be the force, but the goddess is the flow. This perception of goddess is closely related to the Chinese concept of the Tao, the way. Ellen Chen, a scholar of ancient Chinese literature, writes that Taoism grew from very early Chinese beliefs about the Great Mother, once again affirming the perceptions of goddess as Mother Nature—in the sense that she is not so much in each leaf or flower as in the process of their budding, opening and dying, as new buds continually appear on the vine.

In 1978, Susan Griffin wrote that 'many men seem to have an illusion of themselves as being above nature, disconnected even from their own human nature.'

Other women began to question the very concept of a transcendent deity, one that is outside of nature or above it. Patriarchal religions always seem to be looking heavenward, like the worshippers of the sky gods who had originally suppressed the ancient goddess religion. On the other hand, the women in women's spirituality began to look for the Goddess in each other, in themselves, in other animals, in trees and plants, in rivers and oceans. The Goddess of most contemporary women is not 'out there' somewhere. She is the very essence of life, life here on earth:

Mother Nature. So one of the most pressing political issues that those who revere the Goddess are taking on today is the threat to the Goddess herself.

Theologian Dr. Carol Christ is certainly one of those women who think for themselves. She was the co-editor of *Women's Spirit Rising,* and the author of the book *Diving Deep and Surfacing,* as well as many articles including 'Why Women Need the Goddess.'

CAROL CHRIST I think that the conception of God that has come down to us through the traditions of the West has influenced in a subtle way religious studies as an academic discipline—based on a model in which God is separated from humanity and from nature. And we have God on one plane, humanity on a second plane, and nature on the lower plane. With the prehistoric goddesses, I think that you have a much more holistic concept, where God, humanity, and nature are understood to be interlocking dimensions where the Goddess is both nature and woman and something awesome or something holy. I don't think that there's an absolute metaphysical or categorical distinction between goddess, woman, and nature. So it's a very different understanding, and I think that it's really essential that this understanding become incorporated into the way we think about the world, because I think a lot of our ecological problems, a lot of our problems with the threat of nuclear war, come out of this separation of the divinity and morality (associated with the divinity) from nature.

MERLIN STONE Author Marilyn French would certainly agree with Carol Christ on her perceptions of deity. This subject became the focus of her book *Beyond Power,* which was published in 1985.

Marilyn, when you speak of power in the book, you differentiate between the meanings of 'power to' and 'power over.'

MARILYN FRENCH 'Power to' is ability, is talent, is skill involving discipline, and it is a source of tremendous joy. If you look at a little baby when it first takes its steps by itself, you know how wonderful 'power to' feels. Or if you play a musical instrument, if you get that Chopin ballad to sound the way it's supposed to, or if you're an athlete and you make it, if you get that high jump done, you know that 'power to' is a source of enormous pleasure, even though it requires discipline and that involves pain.

'Power over' is domination. What we live in, actually, is a world in which domination has been raised to the highest power. In other words, the meaning of God in most religions in the world is 'power over,' is domination, and God gave humans, in the early part of Genesis, dominion over the  earth and the fish and the flesh and the fowl. Domination has been raised to a divine principle and a God, and people seek it. They seek 'power over' thinking it's going to bring them contentment, invulnerability, safety, happiness; and, of course, it brings misery, and that's all it brings. Isolation, mistrust, separation from others, and just plain unhappiness.

A high god, a transcendent god, is a god of domination, and this is very profound, because it posits an idea that as far as we know is contrary to fact. It posits the idea that there is and can be a power that can move you but be unmoved. An unmoved mover, a god who is above nature, above humans, who can affect them and yet not be affected in return, who is invulnerable, who is impregnable—consider that root—and therefore has a kind of complete domination and yet has invulnerability. Now it is this notion of godhood that is new when patriarchy begins, and, as I've said, it is totally false. Everything that we see in the new physics, in the new science, in the new biology shows that everything is interconnected and everything affects everything else. There is nothing within nature that can move other things without being moved in return. The idea that men have been pursuing is to reach this position where they can affect women, can affect nature, and not be affected in return. And where have they got us?

MERLIN STONE How important do you feel it is for women to be aware and knowledgeable about ancient Goddess worship and the societies in which goddesses were revered?

MARILYN FRENCH Anything that casts aspersions or doubt or turns away from the 'real' God that is worshipped throughout the Western world, and largely in the Eastern world as well, that is, the God of domination, anything that says domination is not good, but there is another way, is helping us, is useful and fruitful.

MERLIN STONE Do you think that that kind of knowledge offers women any assistance in developing the 'power to'—such as to speak, to act, and to question or challenge patriarchical attitudes?

MARILYN FRENCH Absolutely. I think that we have been sold a myth. The myth is that cavemen were even more brutal to their women than men are today. This is hard to believe, because in some places in the world, men are so brutal to women that if they were any more so, there wouldn't be any women. And that things have all improved, from the hair-pulling, grunting days when women were simply dragged into men's caves, to this present day when women are allowed the great luxury of washing dishes and not being hit for it. In fact, our history is different from that. And if you can unearth evidence of Goddess worship, anything that can show women it wasn't always this way, in fact it was far better for women, and that this is an aberration and a deviation, that's good. The most important task of a society is creating the next generation and the world that generation will live in, and you don't do it by stripping the mines and dropping acid in the lakes and all of that. But men still keep trying to place themselves in the image of this god they have devised.

MERLIN STONE In 1970, when every feminist I knew told me that my idea of writing a book about the ancient goddess religion was too removed from the politics of feminism, one woman assured me that if I felt that excited by it, it must be something that needed doing. That woman was Susan Griffin, a poet who later wrote the book *Woman and Nature*.

Susan, you have placed before us in the book some very convincing evidence that males assume they have a right to control and use nature, even to the extent of destroying it.

SUSAN GRIFFIN I feel that men's psychology—and to some degree women's psychology—is split. In fact, in the human experience, it's an inescapable fact that we have to confront every minute that we are material. You get hungry, you get thirsty, you feel a little sleepy, you feel sexual energy. You know that you have an animal nature and that you're dependent on the biosphere in some ways. Your body tells you that. You have to do something

with that part of your nature if
you're going to deny it exists. One
of the things that you can do is
split off, so that you identify
yourself with your intellect, with
the part of you that's dominant
and in control, with the part of
you that you consider spiritual, that
is, transcendent, which is not what
I consider spiritual. That part of
you that feels a mastery over life. The other part, which has needs,
has overwhelming emotions, is very sensual, sometimes doesn't
completely understand everything, feels a little lost, is frightened,
has an awareness of what birth and death are about—that part,
you say that's not me. If you look at those two halves of one person
I've described, you look at a man and a woman. And we are in a
terrible natural crisis because it is men, or it is women who have
those kinds of masculine values because of the nature of the power
system, who are in power now by and large, and it's those people
who are making the decisions. They don't face that in fact we are
part of this biosphere and the biosphere is being destroyed.

MERLIN STONE Do you think women really are closer or more
akin, more in tune with nature?

SUSAN GRIFFIN Well, I think so, absolutely. Yes.

MERLIN STONE Some goddess-revering groups do include men
as well as women. Do you feel that men, at least some men, are
capable of revering or being in touch with nature as fully and
deeply as women are?

SUSAN GRIFFIN Oh yes, I feel certainly that that's true. I think
that men have had a more brutal socialization, and they also have
been given a continual kind of advantage that is more than simply
in the moment saying, 'Well, shall I take this or that.' Because it's
been a continual advantage, it gets more deeply ingrained into
what we think of as their nature. I think it's a harder leap for men
to make, but I don't think it's indelibly biological that men are
separated from nature at all. As a matter of fact, I think what is
indelibly biological is that they're part of nature.

MERLIN STONE   When I spoke with novelist Erica Jong, she mentioned an aspect of contemporary culture that inadvertantly reveals an attitude closely linked to a masculist desire for transcendence.

ERICA JONG   I see an awful lot of 'Let's cast off this planet, it's polluted anyway. Let's go off into outer space.' Movies such as *Cocoon*, books such as Carl Sagan's new novel, *Contact*, seem to posit the notion that we're destroying the earth anyway, so let's go into a pod, blast off into space, and cast off this crummy old planet that's filled with radiation. I don't think that any worshipper of the Goddess would feel that way about the planet.

MERLIN STONE   It's that typical attitude of obsolescence. We use up paper towels and we use up paperbacks and we use up everything we have, and now we've used up the planet, let's go someplace else.

ERICA JONG   Let's go to another one. Now, after a period of Thatcherism and Reaganism rampant in the world, we have to renew our conviction that God can be worshipped in other forms and that female power is really a very spiritual thing.

MERLIN STONE   And the women who follow goddess religion aren't necessarily just simply changing the gender of the deity, but going much beyond that.

ERICA JONG   They're looking at the whole world order in a new way. Inevitably they're bound up with environmentalism, women's control of their own bodies, life preservation rather than dooming the planet to death.

MERLIN STONE   What began as an attempt to tell the truth about ancient goddess worship and a female clergy, to counteract the falsehood of a divine male superiority, has evolved into a philosophical analysis of patriarchal values. The grandest and most glorious images of patriarchal art and literature—the battle hero, the pioneer who cuts down forests or jungles to build great cities, the seeker of immortality—are now seen to be the very images that reveal patriarchal disconnection from the flow and cycles of nature. And this disconnection has led us to the threat of planetary disaster. The return of the Goddess in women's spirituality may be serving the role of the little boy in *The Emperor's New Clothes*. Women are saying, 'Stop this pretence of glory and importance and look at the mess you've made.' Yes, the Goddess has returned, or we have returned to Her. I've often felt that I've heard her voice in my mind. Perhaps it's only my imagination, but I think that what she's saying now is, 'Open your eyes. Look at what you're doing before it's too late.' ◉

SUGGESTED READING

Historical background—Merlin Stone, *When God Was A Woman*, HBJ/Harvest, 1976. Also, *Ancient Mirrors of Womanhood*, Beacon, 1979. Also, Marija Gimbutas, *Goddesses and Gods of Old Europe*, University of California Press, 1974.

Theology—Mary Daly, *Pure Lust*, Beacon, 1973. Also, Carol Christ, *Diving Deep and Surfacing*, Beacon, 1980.

Fiction—Erica Jong, *Fanny*, Signet, 1980.

Psychology—Jean Shinoda Bolen, *Goddesses in Everywoman*, Harper & Row, 1984. Also, Edward Whitmont, *Return of the Goddess*. Crossing Press, 1984.

Feminist/political—Marilyn French, *Beyond Power*, Summit Books, 1985. Also, Susan Griffin, *Woman and Nature*, Harper & Row, 1978.

Pagan religion—Starhawk, *The Spiral Dance*, Harper & Row, 1979. Also, *Dreaming the Dark*, Harper & Row, 1982.

MORE WHERE THIS CAME FROM...

A transcript of the complete four-hour *Return of the Goddess* series, produced by Max Allen and Linda Perry, is available for $5.00 from CBC Enterprises, Box 500, Station A, Toronto, Ontario, Canada MSW lE6.

PAUL TILL

WILD FOODS FIELD GUIDE

Shopping in the forest—a master forager's primer

FOR CENTURIES the value of wild foods has been understood and exploited in Europe, Africa, and the East. Although the pioneers in North America found uses for a dozen uncultivated foods, it is only in recent years that we have rediscovered them. Hundreds of edible wild plants grow in almost any field, forest, marsh or river valley. Here are six of the more common ones that will get you off to a good start.

FIDDLEHEAD *(Matteucia struthiopteris)*

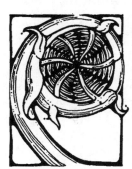

DESCRIPTION: The tightly curled emerging fronds of the ostrich fern, found in river valleys in May. The delicate green croziers, about one inch (2.5 cm) across, are at first covered with a paper-thin brown husk that is readily brushed or shaken free. Historically associated with New Brunswick, fiddleheads grow equally well in several provinces and the northern United States. They are gaining a reputation as a unique wild delicacy, with a pleasant texture and a nutty flavour somewhat like that of asparagus.

HABITAT: In the floodplains of slow-moving rivers and streams where a periodic deposit of sediment is laid down to nourish them.

HOW SERVED: As a steamed or sautéed vegetable, served with butter, vinegar or lemon juice. Also as a component of many recipes, combined with other vegetables, meats, and fish.

STORAGE: As a fresh vegetable, for two weeks in refrigeration. Blanched briefly, they freeze perfectly for future use.

NUTRITION (estimate): 20 to 30% protein. A rich source of niacin, iron, phosphorus, potassium, calcium and vitamins A and C. These ingredients probably account for its reputation as the ideal spring tonic.

CATTAIL SHOOT *(Typha latifolia)*

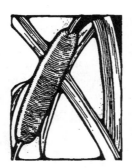

DESCRIPTION: The dominant plant of open marshes, where it grows in large clear stands in shallow water. The leaves are ribbon- or sword-like, one inch (2.5 cm) wide and five feet (1.5 m) long. The fruit is the familiar 'frankfurter' at the top of a stiff, smooth stem. The young male flower (edible) is a green spike above the young female flower. In spring, the male flower quickly bursts with yellow pollen. The rootstalks are two inches (5 cm) thick, growing horizontally just below the surface.

HABITAT: Cattails are the dominant plants of marshes, where they grow to the almost complete exclusion of any other plant.

HOW USED: A rich source of several foods. Probably the best is the male flower, picked while green in spring, cooked as a vegetable and eaten like corn-on-the-cob. In spring, the inner core of the new shoots can be treated like asparagus. The roots may be boiled, washed or dried to make flour. This is the most useful and versatile of all wild food plants.

STORAGE: The male flowers last only a few days before bursting with pollen. The core lasts well in refrigeration, and the roots last indefinitely and can be dried.

NUTRITION (estimate): The male flower is almost entirely pollen, which is about 25% protein. The core and the roots contain large amounts of carbohydrates and trace amounts of several minerals and vitamins.

DANDELION *(Taraxacum officinale)*

DESCRIPTION: This common weed needs no introduction. For salads, the spring leaves must be picked early; if they are picked after the flower buds appear, they are slightly bitter. When picking, cut the thick root below the crown of leaves and remove the overwintering base leaves. Their rich mineral content makes the dandelion leaves both a tasty and a healthful addition to salads.

HABITAT: Anywhere where they can receive large amounts of sunlight and where the soil is not regularly cultivated.

HOW USED: In early spring, use the leaves in mixed green salads. Make tea from the leaves or roots; it has medicinal qualities. In the autumn, the thick roots may be dried and grated for use as a coffee substitute.

STORAGE: In the refrigerator, the leaves keep up to a week, but frequent picking is recommended.

NUTRITION (estimate): The richest plant source of iron and copper. Rich in calcium, phosphorus and vitamins A and C; also contains Vitamin B1, riboflavin, niacin and protein.

ROCKET *(Hesperis matronalis)*

DESCRIPTION: Many members of the cress, or mustard, family have edible leaves that add a lively, spicy quality to a mixed green salad. The best of the group, because of its large cluster of fresh leaves, is rocket or sweet rocket. In the early spring, the rosette of leaves appears in rich soil and wasteland. Each leaf is dark green, lance-shaped and slightly hairy. In June, when the erect flower stem bears white, mauve or pink flowers, the plant resembles garden phlox.

STORAGE: Keeps ten days when fresh in spring. Later, begins to yellow after five days.

Nutrition (estimate): Percentages of major nutrients not known, but recognized as a source of calcium, iron, copper, trace elements and vitamins A and C.

HABITAT: In moist places, usually on the drainage slopes of streams.

HOW USED: As a spicy garnish in green salad in spring. May be steamed briefly as a cooked vegetable.

MORELS *(Morchella esculenta)*

DESCRIPTION: This species and its close relatives are the most sought after of any wild fungi. It is almost impossible to mistake for another mushroom: the conical head resembles a pine cone and is mounted on a thick, white stem. The surface is made up of hollows and ridges; the colour ranges from pale yellow to brown. Cut open, the head and stem are hollow. WARNING: Although this and other true morels are perfectly safe and edible, *the mushroom collector should always check the identity of specimens before using them.*

HABITAT: Morels grow where you find them, and that may be almost anywhere. The most dependable sources, though (no promises!), are in old orchards around the base of decaying trees, and in or along the edges of hardwood forests—especially where the soil has been disturbed.

HOW USED: A gourmet's delight, with a taste that can't be tamed. Excellent in fried butter, or used to add outstanding flavour to meat dishes and casseroles. Generally considered the finest of all edible fungi in Canada, comparable to truffles in Europe.

STORAGE: Fresh specimens keep ten days in refrigerator. Can be frozen or dried and reconstituted.

NUTRITION (estimate): Like most mushrooms, morels contain up to 60% protein. Also a source of several minerals, including trace elements.

WILD LEEK *(Allium tricoccum)*

DESCRIPTION: Two broad green leaves, six inches (15 cm) tall, appear in patches in moist woodlands in April and last until June, when they wither away and the flowerstalk appears. The bulb—up to one inch (2.5 cm) in diameter—is elongated and grows just below the surface of the rich soil. Both the leaves and the bulb are strongly onion-scented. This is without question the best of all wild onions.

HABITAT: Wild leeks usually grow in large patches close to streams or in moist areas in hardwood forests, particularly under the cover of sugar maples.

HOW SERVED: Both leaves and bulb are used to garnish salads. Both may be used as a cooked vegetable. The bulbs make a thick, aromatic, delicate soup. Considered by many to be unrivalled as a soup base.

STORAGE: Early in the season both leaves and bulb keep well in refrigeration if separated and kept dry with paper towelling. By late May the leaves turn yellow and age quickly. The bulbs keep for weeks or can be frozen for soups.

NUTRITION (estimate): Similar to other onions. Protein 10 to 15%. Rich in iron, calcium and vitamins A and C. ◉

JULIA BLUSHAK

CAMPING AT WALDEN POND

A fresh look at Thoreau's *Life in the Woods*

IT IS HARD, maybe impossible, for any child raised in the raging blizzard of signals to find his way back into the exacting silence of a book. *Walter Benjamin, 1948*

THESE DAYS it's hard to concentrate, and many of us don't like the exacting silence of books. Instead, we drop ideas into our conversations even if we haven't actually read the authors who conceived of them. It isn't always a problem; sometimes it's good. In this way, ideas become popular, part of an oral tradition independent of their authors. Thus, revolutionary ideas like the Oedipus complex or the hundredth monkey phenomenon enter our vocabulary, if not our library.

On the down side, writers can be abused or misunderstood when their thought is reduced to this form. We all know what Hitler did with the rumour of Nietzsche's 'super man.' By this process, the genetic subtleties of Darwin's theory of natural selection were reduced to the vicious notion of the survival of the fittest, a pseudo-scientific rationalization for every kind of selfishness.

When people talk about getting back—or even *forward*—to Nature, poor old Henry Thoreau often suffers from the bad side of this rumour syndrome. The word 'Walden' has come to be shorthand for the Mother Nature we have lost; it evokes a longing tinged with escapism, for a mythic landscape as remote as Camelot. To redress this imbalance, I propose that we take a fresh look at *Walden*, to see what Thoreau really thought of Mother Nature.

WALDEN; *or, Life in the Woods* was published over 130 years ago, in 1854—five years before Darwin's *Origin of Species*, six years after Marx's *Communist Manifesto*, and two years before the birth of Sigmund Freud. The book is an account of the way of life that Thoreau pursued for two years, living alone in a shack that he built for himself on the shores of Walden Pond, near Concord, Massachusetts. It is an inquiry into the relation between the way we live and who we are; that is, in a moral sense, what kind of human beings we are. Where many imagine *Walden* to be a natural idyll, it is actually a work of cantankerous and austere philosophy, written out of a deep affinity for the most ascetic teachings of the ancient world, especially of the Greek Pythagoreans and the Indian Sanskrit texts.

Thoreau lived on coarse unleavened bread and water, gruel, and occasional fish. He passed the time observing nature, going out of his way to visit particular trees and groves of black birch, beech, or hemlock, which he revered as shrines of pilgrimage. 'I went to the woods,' he declares, 'because I wished to live deliberately, to front only the essential facts of life, and see if I could learn what it had to teach, and not, when I came to die, discover that I had not lived. I did not wish to live what was not life, living is so dear; nor did I wish to practice resignation, unless it was quite necessary. I wanted to live deep and suck all the marrow out of life . . . to drive life into a corner, and reduce it to its lowest terms, and, if it proved mean, why then to get the whole and genuine meanness out of it, and publish its meanness to the world; or if it were sublime, to know it by experience.'

Thoreau's observations on mankind are often tinged with anger and contempt, but occasionally with an irony worthy of Jonathan Swift: 'I believe that men are generally still a little afraid of the dark, though the witches are all hung, and Christianity and candles have been introduced.' He has no patience with consensus morality. 'The greatest part of what my neighbours call good I believe in my soul to be bad, and if I repent anything, it is very likely to be my good behaviour.'

His non-conformist credo is haunting and appealing, yet remote to many of us. It seems like a voice from the immediate past—from the '60s—rather than from the 1850s. This isn't so strange, really, because the influence of Thoreau, along with

Emerson and Whitman, resonates through all the arts in America. It can be traced via performers such as Woody Guthrie to Bob Dylan and all of his generation of artists. Remember John Prine's 'Spanish Pipedream'? 'Blow up your TV, throw away your paper, go to the country, build you a home.' Thoreau's observations on conventional wisdom are as irreverent and pungent as any Prine ballad: 'As for the Pyramids, there is nothing to wonder at in them so much as the fact that so many men could be found degraded enough to spend their lives constructing a tomb for some ambitious booby, whom it would have been wiser and manlier to have drowned in the Nile and then given his body to the dogs.'

Very early on in the book, he expresses proto-feminist sympathies, in an extraordinary comment that is at once glib and profound. 'Think, also, of the ladies of the land weaving toilet cushions against the last day, not to betray too green an interest in their fates! As if you could kill time without injuring eternity.' What an extraordinary thing for a man to say in New England in 1854! He seems to hold women responsible for their destinies when they didn't even have the vote, much less the freedom to find their Walden; when women were still considered to be the property of their menfolk, with marginally more privilege and independence than favourite slaves. Although he says little else about women in the book, clearly he encourages them as much as men to stop abusing themselves with unconscious drudge work: 'A simple and independent mind does not toil at the bidding of any prince. Through want of enterprise and faith men are where they are, buying and selling, and spending their lives like serfs.'

You may have heard that Thoreau was just a bum who didn't want to look for honest work. True, he champions idleness, but only to be free to meditate. 'No method nor discipline can supersede the necessity of being forever on the alert. I did not read books the first summer; I hoed beans. Nay, I often did better than this. There were times when I could not afford to sacrifice the bloom of the present moment to any work, whether of the head or hands . . . I grew in those seasons like corn in the night, and they were far better than any work of the hands would have been.' As in the work of Proust, no detail of perception is too trivial for his pen. His description of the 'behaviour' of bubbles under the winter ice is as fascinating as any astronomer's revelations of supernovas.

People have also said that Thoreau exaggerates his isolation, that he poses as a woodsman while staying quite close to town. Actually, he is quite frank about this. His nearest neighbour was a mile away. His purpose being to live alone with his thoughts, his Walden didn't need to be wilderness, but simply clean, uncultivated, and uninhabited. However, it may come as a bit of a shock to learn that, contrary to what purists might expect of him, this folk hero of the Green Movement went to town almost every day 'to hear some of the gossip.' Clearly, he needed the contact as therapy against cabin fever, but he justified it to himself differently: he compares the villagers to a colony of prairie dogs whose habits interested him.

During his time squatting at Walden, Thoreau cultivated a couple of acres of beans to sell, practising the most rudimentary husbandry without horse, plough, or manure. What for most of us would be boring as hell was for him high drama reminiscent of *The Iliad*: '. . . a long war with weeds, those Trojans who had sun and rain and dews on their side. Daily the beans saw me come to their rescue armed with a hoe, and thin the ranks of their enemies, filling up the trenches with weedy dead.' His views on what is necessary to sustain health are entertaining, even to a hardened carnivore like me: 'One farmer said, "You cannot live on vegetable food solely, for it furnishes nothing to make bones with," walking all the while behind his oxen, which, with vegetable-made bones, jerk him and his lumbering plow along in spite of every obstacle.' Although he calls flesh-eating 'unclean,' he's not religious about it, nor 'unusually squeamish'—no Bambi complex here. He 'could sometimes eat a fried rat with relish, if it were necessary.'

At the slightest provocation, his bile rises against the mercantile instinct, condemning brute selfishness in the marketplace. It is an intermittent misanthropy, like that of an Old Testament prophet who condemns us for our own good. 'White Pond and Walden are great crystals on the surface of the earth. If they were

permanently congealed, and small enough to be clutched, they would, perchance, be carried off by slaves, like precious stones, to adorn the heads of emperors; talk of heaven! ye disgrace earth.' Here's my favourite among his diatribes against utilitarianism: 'And now the villagers, who scarcely know where it lies, instead of going to the pond to bathe or drink, are thinking to bring its water, which should be as sacred as the Ganges at least, to the village in a pipe, to wash their dishes with!—to earn their Walden by the turning of a cock or drawing of a plug! Where is the Moore of Moore Hall, to meet the enemy at the Deep Cut and thrust an avenging lance between the ribs of the bloated pest?' Perhaps it's good for Thoreau that so much of his reputation rests on hearsay. It is comfortable to make casual reference to his back-to-nature vision, but to really know it by careful reading is to be chastened, or else to reject it for the perversity of his self-denial, which is as repugnant to most of us as the discipline of the Jain ascetic who lived on just one ju-ju bean a day.

What a deep resounding puritan you are, Henry! Very like a Buddhist monk, really, yet also like a Rastafarian among the fruit trees of Ja: 'I did not use tea, nor coffee, nor butter, nor milk, nor fresh meat, and so did not have to work hard to get them; and again, as I did not work hard, I did not have to eat hard, and it cost me but a trifle for my food.'

Though he preaches sobriety, we can only wonder what sensitizing drugs he could have found in the woods that would provoke such enchanting and unlikely visions as his description of the end of the rainbow: 'Once it chanced that I stood in the very abutment of a rainbow's arch, which filled the lower stratum of the atmosphere, tingeing the grass and leaves all around, and dazzling me. It was a lake of rainbow light, in which, for a short while, I lived like a dolphin.'

Living at Walden, Thoreau discovered in himself, at times, a desire to kill and eat game, though he had sold his gun before he went to the woods, and despite his conscious abstinence from meat. He reveres this instinct as essential to his humanity, evidence of higher laws. 'When some of my friends have asked me anxiously about their boys, whether they should let them hunt, I have answered, yes,—remembering that it was one of the best parts of my education—*make* them hunters. There is a period in the history of the individual, as of the race, when hunters are the "best men", as the Algonquins called them.' Thoreau provides an elegant explanation for the power and authenticity of, for example, William Faulkner's stories of hunting initiation in the Deep South. It is not simply an uncivilized macho habit. He argues convincingly (at least to an ex-hunter like me) that the hunter stage is a necessary aspect of adolescence, which one loses the taste for with maturity of conscience. Sadly, he notes, 'The mass of men are still and always young in this respect.'

He is very thoughtful about the contradictions between his empirical observations and his philosophical inclinations vis-à-vis non-injury, vegetarianism, and other oriental ideals that he espouses while condoning the hunting and eating of game: 'The particular laws [of Nature] are as our points of view, as to the traveller, a mountain outline varies with every step, and it has an infinite number of profiles, though absolutely but one form. Even when cleft or bored through it is not comprehended in its entireness.'

If we are wondering, as we read, what on earth Henry does for sex, he eventually gets around to telling us—he doesn't. He's chaste. This is a discipline very much in vogue these days as perhaps it has never been since 1854, and might have ensured *Walden*'s tenure on the *New York Times Bestseller List*. Unfortunately, he doesn't say much about it, except to observe wistfully that 'our whole life is startlingly moral.'

The most perverse analogy in *Walden* is one that reveals the tragic aspect of Thoreau's psychology, the tragedy of the cerebral man, the Idealist: 'Why is it that a bucket of water soon becomes putrid, but frozen remains sweet forever? It is commonly said that this is the difference between the affections and the intellect.' That the affections, which may both motivate and give value to sex, generation, and the process of nurturing between parent and child, should be denigrated by analogy as *putrid!*

Yet, complementing this dark side, he has extraordinary sensibilities, nowhere more acute than in the ecstatic 'crisis' of spring: 'The change from storm and winter to serene and mild weather, from dark and sluggish hours to bright and elastic ones, is a memorable crisis which all things proclaim. Suddenly an influx of light filled my house.' At his best, he sings the necessity of organic *conscience*, insisting that life in the woods is soul-making: '*we need the tonic of wildness.*' *Walden* challenges us to know ourselves, not by travel, nor by vain ambition, but by opening 'new channels, not of trade, but of thought. It is not worth the while to go round the world to count the cats in Zanzibar.'

Thoreau would rather spend an eternity in hell than five minutes in the company of a fool, and he calls most of his neighbours foolish; he is pompous, and never was as free of civilization as he often leads the reader to imagine. But the book is a great delight, and deserves the reputation that has made its rumour so popular. It remains a handbook for sympathetic souls, to inflame the adventurous and enlighten the duty-bound. ◉

MARSHALL MCLUHAN PHOTOGRAPHED BY JOHN REEVES

In Praise of Walking

Early one morning, any morning, we can set out, with the least possible baggage, and discover the world.

It is quite possible to refuse all the coercion, violence, property, triviality, to simply walk away.

That something exists outside ourselves and our preoccupations, so near, so readily available, is our greatest blessing.

Walking is the human way of getting about.

Always, everywhere, people have walked, veining the earth with paths, visible and invisible, symmetrical or meandering.

There are walks on which we tread in the footsteps of others, walks on which we strike out entirely for ourselves.

A journey implies a destination, so many miles to be consumed, while a walk is its own measure, complete at every point along the way.

There are things we will never see, unless we walk to them.

Walking is a mobile form of waiting.

What I take with me, what I leave behind, are of less importance than what I discover along the way.

To be completely lost is a good thing on a walk.

The most distant places seem accessible once one is on the road.

Convictions, directions, opinions, are of less importance than sensible shoes.

In the course of a walk we usually find out something about our companion, and this is true even when we travel alone.

When I spend a day talking I feel exhausted, when I spend it walking I am pleasantly tired.

The pace of a walk will determine the number and variety of things to be encountered, from the broad outlines of a mountain range to a tit's nest among the lichen, and the quality of attention that will be brought to bear upon them.

A rock outcrop, a hedge, a fallen tree, anything that turns us out of our way, is an excellent thing on a walk.

Wrong turnings, doubling back, pauses and digressions, all contribute to the dislocation of a persistent self interest.

Everything we meet is equally important or unimportant.

The most lonely places are the most lovely.

Walking is egalitarian and democratic; we do not become experts at walking and one side of the road is as good as another.

Walking is not so much romantic as reasonable.

The line of a walk is articulate in itself, a kind of statement.

We lose the flavour of walking if it becomes too rare or too extraordinary, if it turns into an expedition; rather it shoud be quite ordinary, unexceptional, just what we do.

Daily walking, in all weathers, in every season, becomes a sort of ground or continuum upon which the least emphatic occurrences are registered clearly.

A stick of ash or blackthorn, through long use, will adjust itself to the palm.

Of the many ways through a landscape, we can choose, on each occasion, only one, and the project of the walk will be to remain responsive, adequate, to the consequences of the choice we have made, to confirm the chosen way rather than refuse the others.

One continues on a long walk not by an effort of will but through fidelity.

Storm clouds, rain, hail, when we have survived these we seem to have taken on some of the solidity of rocks or trees.

A day, from dawn to dusk, is the natural span of a walk.

A dull walk is not without value.

To walk for hours on a clear night is the largest experience we can have.

For the right understanding of a landscape, information must come to the intelligence from all the senses.

Climbing uphill, the horizon grows wider; descending, the hills gather round.

We can take a walk which is a sampling of different airs: the invigorating air of the heights; the filtered air of a pine forest; the rich air over ploughed earth.

We can walk between two places and in so doing establish a link between them, bring them into a warmth of contact, like introducing two friends.

There are walks on which I lose myself, walks which return me to myself again.

Is there anything that is better than to be out, walking, in the clear air?

HUNGER BY FIONA SMYTH

ENOUGH ABOUT THE PHALLUS!

THE STUDY OF LITERATURE has devoted an entire school to 'anything that is longer than it is wide.' Historians look for phallic symbols in folklore and mythology. Psychologists have a field day with phallo-centricity, penis envy, and dreams of sprouting volcanoes and tall buildings.

Children are indoctrinated early in life. The penis is the most noticeable part of the male body; therefore, it must bear significance in other bodies of work. I can still remember the joy I felt when I identified my first phallic symbol in a book that I was reading for junior high school. But soon enough, the pillar of symboldom became unenticing. I became sick of the eager college student pining about phallic symbols. Surely other parts of the male body had as much meaning.

Enter the scrotum. Despite being overshadowed by the phallus, the scrotum exceeds the phallus both aesthetically and in the amount of symbolic references it suggests. Although recently the phallus has gained the upper hand in its popularity, historically, before Sigmund Freud, the scrotum was the height of erotic interest. Even industry was captivated by the scrotum. The umbrella was inspired by the scrotum; so were the shopping bag, tea cup, and balloon. In Greek and Roman times, special handshakes existed to ritually celebrate the hidden symbol. Today, the International Friends of the Scrotum are keeping these handshakes alive. Their founder, the inventor of Le Bag and Hacky Sack, has created a fund for academics interested in researching the scrotum and scrotic symbols, i.e., Scrotic Studies.

Already, in the finer institutions in the United States and France, where tight jeans have always displayed the scrotum's superior attractiveness, students are beginning to talk about scrotic symbols: No longer can the sight of a man twist-tying bulging green garbage bags, carrying two of them out the door and placing them on the sidewalk for the garbageman to hoist into the powerful incinerating dump truck, be considered devoid of symbolic scrotic meaning. Nor can the interaction between the housewife and checkout boy exchanging shopping bags be anything but a well-established scrotic ritual.

The Moon, the Sun, the Earth—these are the great scrotic symbols. Early humans worshipped them. They built wide, round, bulbous habitats, not skyscrapers. The scrotum is round and contains two equal orbs. Although physiologically the clitoris and penis are similar, symbolically the clitoris is more akin to the scrotum than to the long skinny phallus. Thus, for Marxists and/or feminists, the scrotum can be interpreted as anti-capitalist and anti-egocentric. Scrotic housing is communal and does not yield high profits because it is not as space efficient as the skyscraper.

The scrotum is a more universal symbol than the individualistic phallus. Ziplock bags can hold an entire world in their grasp, whereas the unencompassing phallus merely droops like aged celery.

Despite a recent Roper poll showing that 60 percent of the women surveyed find the scrotum more attractive than the phallus, the scrotum has a long way to go. It is still a bold act for a student to ask if bumper cars, basketballs or bald men with wigs are scrotic symbols. Until the scrotum can be accepted in the cloistered circles of academia, the International Friends of the Scrotum and other scrotic admirers must practise their two special age-old handshakes in secret: the first, cupping hands together, like the 'Good Hands' people, and placing them on the partner's cupped hands; the second, cupping the partner's right fist in your left hand, and placing your right fist in the partner's left hand.

The phallus has been the centre of attention for too long and its days are numbered. The scrotum is a better symbol and will open an entire untapped world for academia and industry. The Russians, intrigued by the scrotum for years, are pouring money into Scrotic Studies.* They know too well that phallo-centric minds have produced enough dangerous weapons. Support the scrotum. It is a well-known universal symbol of world peace and will bring warmth and security to an uptight, phallo-centric world.   ◎

* They call it Scroticheski Otdelenye. More information can be found in the popular Soviet journal *Scrotichiya Cevodnya* (roughly translated as 'Scrotum Today').

MERCURE
_____

POIS(S)ON

HESITATING
_____

RU(M)INATION

HOOKED
_____

ADDI(C)TIVE

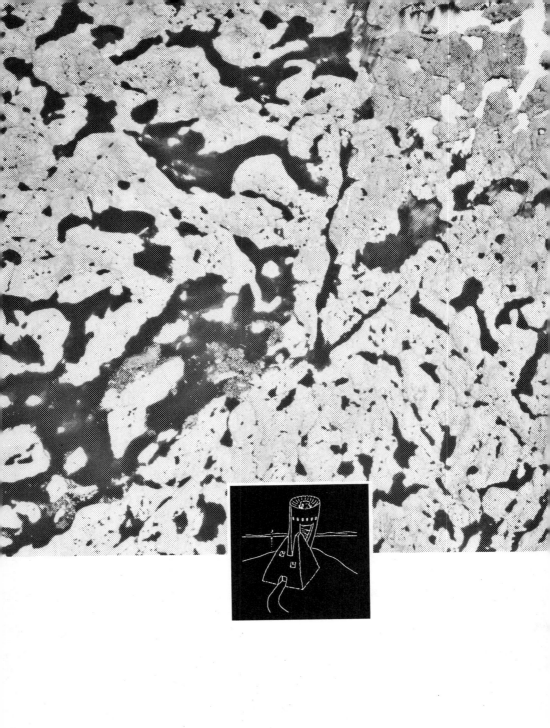

NORTHERN LIGHTS

EVERY THOUSAND YEARS, a new millenium approaches—relentless like a glacier, invisible like some shifting temporal tectonic plate. Every thousand years, the question must be confronted: What is to be done?

1. PRO TEMPORE

The wind rushed down from the Pole and dropped a feather in my lap. *Explorer, Gulf of Boothia, 1889*

CANADA IS NOT A LARGE NATION. Here and there, fragments of population nestle against the water's edge, staring into distances where population fades into echoes. But Canada is a large country, a vast construct of rock and sap.

Seen from above, the country spreads from the great fat waistband of the 49th parallel, heading northward to slip under the ice of the high Arctic. It is a country of North.

North is a philosophical, even an emotional, stance. It is an ineluctable geographic condition. It means, perhaps, a sense of being at the top of the world—or near enough to smell twenty kinds of snow.

It implies clear vision, not untempered with precarious balance. It may even mean a sensation, felt beneath the skin, of both strength and delicacy, held together in a bond of taciturnity. It means North.

The North was long ago imagined as inaccessible, lodged behind an angry border country. It was known in Greek myth as Hyperborea, the region beyond the birthplace of Boreas—the North Wind. Hyperborea was brushed with gentle breezes that rustled through trees laden with winter fruit. The people were of gentle temperament and given to contemplation.

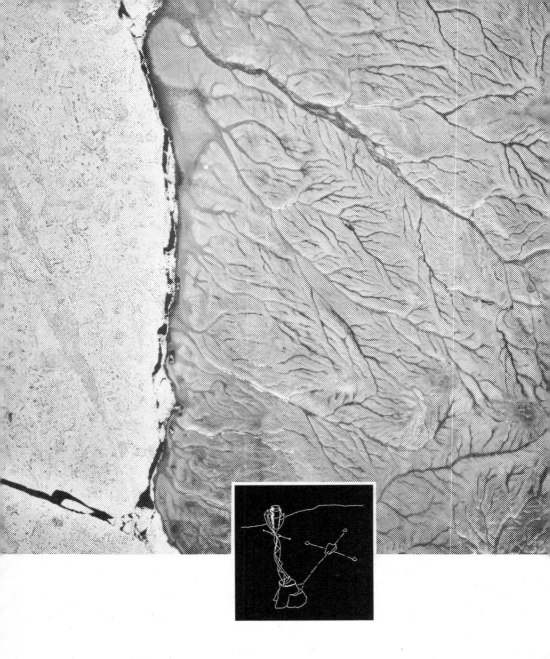

THE NORTH POLE . . . A HUGE
DARK COLUMN OF BASALT
RISING OUT OF GLOOMY SEAS.

Others have regarded the North with horror, as a place of violent spiritual entropy, the home of the Antichrist, a wasteland of curdled will and tumescent evil.

It is neither the one nor the other. It is something of both: a powerful place and a powerful state of mind. Arithmetic would suggest that it is therefore doubly powerful—worth celebrating in its raw presence, and its mythic sinew and size and promise.

And a new millenium is approaching.

2. EX LUMINIS, LUMEN

The stars peered through a web of cloud tonight. We were heartily glad to see them after all that we'd endured.

Navigator, Winisk River, 1906

THE EARTH OFFERS an indifferent face to the skies. It is pocked with cities, lined with coursing transits that have worried the surface like burst capillaries. An unintended face, vastly elaborated.

It may be that the next millenium will shape and clarify this face—lend rigour and intent to some of its features. Consider this: Canada has an area of almost 10 million square kilometres. An international coordinate grid of latitude and longitude lies across this land mass as it does across every point on earth—a fine cartographical mesh.

The grid is objective, perfectly detached. The North is grandly abstract, a compound of inlets, peninsulas, islands adrift in crooked bays, stony promontories. The one rests upon the other like a gentle call to order.

From 45° to 80°N and from 55° to 130°W, there are 86 points at which 5° intervals of latitude and longitude intersect; the objective definition of Canada, of North. As dots on a map, these points suggest some underlying mental web with which to gain purchase on the region's size and weight.

The points fall on all manner of landscape—at Cape Whittle, Lac La Ronge, Egg River, Blackhead Island, Radstock Bay, Forrest Station, Canon Fjord, Byam Channel, Chorkbak Inlet, Flat Sound, Eureka.

AT EACH OF THE 86 POINTS,
THERE IS A LIGHT,
A BEACON TO THE SKY.

Now consider this: At each of the 86 points, there is to be a light. The source of the light—powerful and sharp enough to be distinguished from the encompassing luminous noise in the air—is to be the same at all points: a huge spout of electromagnetic radiation, a beacon to the sky and all who sail in it.

The setting, or housing, for the light—a tower cobbled together from rough stones gathered on the surrounding Shield, a slender frame of old steel from a lake steamer, a flat bed of moss and concrete spread between the cusps of a rocky upcropping through sour muskeg—is to be different at each of the 86 points, each one a single address in an austere and far-flung northern metropolis of lights.

The light setting is to be a firm architectonic presence on the land. The North, after all, is a presence full of presences—the North Pole itself was once thought to be a huge dark column of basalt rising out of gloomy seas.

Each light setting is to be put together by a project team drawn from the region of the light, a region that may extend over enormous distances. The construction of each intersection of the coordinate grid is to be filtered through the region's history, articulated with local materials, pinned to the country's fabric with a light. The grid will meet the landscape with a small metaphysical impact.

The distribution of lights and power will call upon traditions of long-distance communications and transportation, of brave engineering, of overcoming odds and doubters.

From above, from far above, where all future occupants of the sky will see them, the lights will put the North luminously in its place against the vast earthly tapestry. They will be Northern Lights.

THE PATTERN OF LIGHT
MIGHT SUGGEST A GLOBAL
COHERENCE OF ASPIRATIONS.

3. POST HOC

The sun was rising behind the northern peak. We could see the glow around the edges like a masked fire. My companion said it was the dawning of a new day. I said, 'A new age'.

Climber, Beartooth Mountain, 1945

THE NORTHERN LIGHTS will be ignited at one second after midnight on the first day of January in the year 2000. That is, the lights on the east coast will be turned on first and, for the next 5 1/2 hours, the march of pillars of light will proceed west, accompanying the march of time.

It can be foreseen that there will be more lights on more towers, columns, and cairns if other regions uncover the power of the grid on their own landscape, and draw their own images against the sky.

The coordinate grid stretches around the world. There would seem no reason that a pattern of light might not follow, might not suggest, a global coherence of landscape and emotional markings— more strongly, strangely put: a coherence of aspirations.

But Northern Lights will first be eight years in the making. There will be a scramble for funding from governments, corporations, and citizens, and an immense effort of planning and execution—an adventure against time and wilderness. The adventure will justify the scramble, and it will be undertaken lightheartedly.

Then Northern Lights will greet the next millenium with a picture of the country graven upon itelf—a gesture, in the end, of self-respect, of self-possession.

We swept over Kincolith Light, looked down on Kloch Lake Light, and headed for Kugaluk River. The lights below spread a map for us against the night.

Traveller, the North, 2138

◉

Northern Lights is undertaken as part of a series of initiatives intended to transform ideas into places, objects, and sensations, produced by Peter Ferguson, John Ferguson, Christopher Pommer, Anne Sinclair, and Paula Bowley, members of Premises, the research division of Ferguson Ferguson Architects, Toronto. Produced with the assistance of Bernard Stockl Design and Imtek Imagineering Inc.

BARBARA KLUNDER

DELIVERING THE MALE

MY COPY OF IT IS YELLOWING NOW. I've been saving it for ten years, not only because it was a male friend's first ('maiden?') fling into big-league journalism but also because I must have realized, even then, that this was going to be a *big* issue in our lives. The relic I'm referring to is a copy of *Saturday Night* magazine. On its cover is a big closeup of the tear running down a man's face, and the caption: 'Casualties in the age of feminism.'[1] The piece is a pretty unsettling survey of sex-role reversals in the late '60s and early '70s.

I say 'unsettling' because, as promising as it then looked for men—this man, anyway—to 'feminize' themselves, it hasn't altogether worked. We softened, sure enough. We learned, and this was essential, how not to hurt others. We started to identify and indict what the American poet Robert Bly calls 'the Aristotelian and Christian arrogance toward other cultures, toward animals and oceans.' Not to mention women.

This realization wasn't new; it had been going on in the male conscience for more than two hundred years. Among the first poets to sing about the problem—and the solutions—were the English High Romantics such as William Blake, and later many others, for example, Rainer Maria Rilke, D.H. Lawrence, and Walt Whitman.

And so men began to listen as women finally spoke of their experience. A few did a *lot* of listening. But somewhere along the line many of us lost touch with our *own* experience, our own modes of feeling, our own purpose. We became, as Bly put it, 'life-preserving, but not exactly life-*giving*.'

About five years ago, Bly and the psychologist James Hillman began to conduct workshops to 're-vision,' in Hillman's words, what it means to be a man. They began to offer American men an opportunity to become the kind of men their ancestors were, without giving up their hard-won conscience and compassion. Specifically, to find within themselves the mythological character of the Wild Man.

From the epic of *Gilgamesh* to the Grimms' tale *Iron John* to *Sir Gawain and the Green Knight*, the Wild Man is primal male power. He has a quality that's neither savage nor macho, but 'fierce,' a quality men need in order to realize their true masculine strength and use it wisely.

The Wild Man, it must be said, is not 'nice.' He does not conform to society's idea of acceptable behaviour. Rather, he stands, says Bly, 'for the primitive, spontaneous, truthful part of the man, which is historically connected to the hunter and to man's ancient relationship to wild animals.'

In September 1988, I met with a hundred men at a camp in the Minnesota woods to listen as Bly, Hillman, and other tribal 'elders' talked about finding passion and purpose in our lives. To do this, we invoked the image of the Wild Man. We chanted, drummed, made masks, danced, and told stories. What follows is excerpted from talks given over the course of five days, which were then distilled for an hour-long documentary on CBC Radio's *Ideas*.

These men talk about courage; but not the courage to wage wars of aggression. They praise the courage, rather, to recognize both the fiend and the deprived child inside themselves.

ROBERT BLY The Wild Man is normally discussed during our conferences in relation to five other 'Joys' of men: the king, the warrior, the trickster, the lover, and the quester. All of these represent possibilities that a man may develop. After age 35, it seems that the time comes to live these joys consciously. A man may look, for example, at how much genuine king he has in his life. Ordinarily, if he allows other people to initiate a project, or thought, or system, then he doesn't have much king.

During this particular conference we'll concentrate on the ashamed, angry, or disappointed little boy who acts usually to block the expression or development of any one of these Joys. Similarly, women sense that the disappointed or ashamed little girl in them can block the development of their queen or wild woman, or female warrior, and so on.

We're going to begin by learning a little Blake poem. Are you ready for this?

> My mother groan'd! my father wept.
> Into the dangerous world I leapt[2]

Your mother's groaning in the beginning is proper, isn't it— to begin with that? Then it goes to the father, and what the father does is weep. Part of that is from the tradition that your soul came from another place. It was dry up there, and here it's wet. The tradition is that when you come down here, you put on a watery envelope that's called the body. Your father was in touch with that spiritual world; he came from there himself. And when your mother groaned, she was not in touch with it. But he was, and he weeps that you were born at all. Is that clear? Let's continue:

> Helpless, naked, piping loud:
> Like a fiend hid in a cloud.

The 'fiend' is the wild little soul, hidden in the cloud of the body. So this is not Hallmark sentimentality about a little baby. This boy is dangerous, from the first moment he's born. But he's bound, too.

> Struggling in my father's hands,
> Striving against my swaddling bands,
> Bound and weary I thought best
> To sulk upon my mother's breast.

That's a *genius* poem. I don't know how many times I'm in that mood, and I think everything considered, the most rational thing to do is just to sulk: not answer my wife, just sulk. Is that right?

So, one way you can think about that is, 'Who is it in me that's doing the thinking?' There's an adult in you doing it, when you're lucky. And then, more and more, I'm aware of a three-year-old in me. He never got beyond three. He makes up his mind by then that the world is a hostile and strange place. And he holds on to that opinion, often against the evidence, so that when the 35-year-old wants to change his life, to break out, he gets fouled up by the kid inside who's still brooding about the birthday party that didn't work out. The same three-year-old rears his head disastrously in arguments with women.

Your exercise here is to write down the conclusions that that child came to when he was faced with death. Sentences like: 'It is better to pretend I am not who I am than to die.' 'Better to be unmanly or unheroic, and to sulk rather than to lose the mother's breast entirely.' Or, 'It's better to get sick than to go out into the world and die.'

The child in us is so strong that he may actually control the body and health. In my case, the three-year-old would give me a sore throat and a fever two days before I had to give a poetry reading. What's required for men is that we hear that child and listen to him. Tell the little boy that he's made up his mind on the basis of inadequate information. Name his fear. Talk to him.

In my case I said, 'Listen, I went to California in 1956, I was there for six days, I didn't die. I went to New Jersey—remember that time?—in 1961. It was New Jersey, I still didn't die.' I went through a whole series, and said to him, 'Where were you when these things happened? I did not die. I'm alive right now.' And it was interesting, because he hadn't really heard about it. And I was astounded. Within ten minutes, my throat was fine, and my fever was completely gone. That was a lesson to me. I just could not believe that.

TIM WILSON When the boy child sulks at the breast, he chooses self-pity and isolation. He may do this well into adolescence by looking for female comfort. If he is criticized at this point, he may sulk for two or three days. He removes himself from engagement in life, from what Blake describes as fierce and direct perception. This kind of man grows up isolated and jealous. He has the kind of passivity, Bly would say, you get from merely reading these poems instead of singing them, as Blake himself did. And so we sing together:

> Whate'er is Born of Mortal Birth
> Must be consumed with the Earth
> To rise from Generation free:
> Then what have I to do with thee?[3]

ROBERT BLY It's Jesus, of course, who speaks that last line to his mother, at the wedding at Cana. She said, you know, 'Would you mind turning this water into wine? We didn't get to the K-Mart and we didn't buy enough wine.' She knows he can do it, I mean, there's no question about that. And his answer was one that Blake noticed, 'Woman, what have I to do with thee?' Let's carry on:

> Thou, Mother of my Mortal part,
> With cruelty didst mould my Heart,
> And with false self-deceiving tears
> Didst bind my Nostrils, Eyes, & Ears;

What's she doing here? She's being an accomplice to mortality. In the womb, Blake is saying, our souls become trapped in the 'watery envelope' of the body. The mother, by giving us mere nostrils, eyes, and ears, closes off the myriad 'senses' that Blake believed the soul has before it is incarnate in 'senseless clay.'

The cruelty is that this happened to her, and she's pretending she doesn't notice it. She's saying, 'Oh, look at that wonderful little baby. Oh, so good. Aren't you glad I brought you into this world?' That's called false, self-deceiving tears.

TIM WILSON What's being spoken of here is something that happens to everyone on this planet; it is impersonal. The 'universal mother' betrays us. So, too, does each of our personal mothers, though without knowing it, and even though she may be deeply loving. This, Bly suggests, is one meaning of the passage in the Gnostic *Gospel of Thomas* in which Christ says, 'My mother gave me death, but my father gave me life.' We are speaking to our 'mothers,' then, when we address the sulking, soft-seeking parts of ourselves. It is a very difficult but important paradox. To take charge of your life, Bly is saying, this kind of severity may be necessary. But he is not saying that we must be cruel to our own mothers.

ROBERT BLY Let's do this:

> Didst close my Tongue in senseless clay,
> And me to Mortal Life betray.
> The Death of Jesus set me free:
> Then what have I to do with thee?

I want you to do the last stanza, especially the last sentence, and this time I want you to get your voice rough. You don't have to do this to your own mother, but you need to be able to do it to the universe, and not with a soft, little, gentle voice.

TIM WILSON So we sing it out again, loudly. And every one of us is exhilarated by the power that we are finding in ourselves.

JAMES HILLMAN In my own life, the terribly needy little boy is always there, and when I get massaged, for example, he lives in my arms. I always feel the puniness in there. When those places are touched, I feel that little, tiny boy with his thin little neck on the New Jersey beaches where I grew up, trying to keep this head on. Unable to hold that head, with these weak arms that couldn't do it, couldn't do it. It's abso-

lutely crucial that we remember neediness, puniness like that. I mean, you don't need to remember it, because it comes up and grabs you and pulls you down. But very often, it is a root of divorce—'she couldn't give me what I needed.' And it's a root of child abuse. You can't bear the child screaming for attention, and so you beat it up. Owning the need is absolutely the first step, no question about it. But you have to be careful not to stay at the first step. It is absolute, and it is always literal. In order to own something, you have to say, 'I am that little boy.' It's literal and it's monotheistic. 'I am only that little boy.' You lose all the other parts, you forget all the rest of it. It's also very salvational, and very simple: 'If only she would do this; if only I could find a father, or my father; if only my mother hadn't done that.' What you're saying is, 'I am like this, and if only I had that, it would all be solved.'

Now that's a place of being stuck. But what we do instead of owning the need is deny it. Denial is something psychotherapy tries to get rid of. It's regarded as a defence mechanism, and you have to go through it. We feel shame over the weakness as part of the boy child. You don't want to be weak, you don't want to be silent, you don't want to be impotent, you don't want to be incompetent, you don't want to be inadequate, and you feel all of those things. And then you feel ashamed, which makes it even worse.

Instead of that, or along with that, suppose you let the need come up fully. I mean, into its absurdity. Let it express itself fully. Speak it out loud. It's very important to let things come out aloud. Not just sitting in your room and thinking about what you need, or tossing and turning in the night. You say it, 'I want,' you cry it out. You hear it come out of your own throat.

It's not that men are 'just little boys,' but that we have little boys who'll teach us amazing things. For that, though, we have to be there for them, father them, listen to them when they say, 'I don't want to be here alone anymore,' or 'I can't do this without help from someone.' It's the sort of thing you hear in country and western songs—'hurtin' songs.' Letting that voice speak, in Jungian psychology, is the beginning of 'active imagination.'

It seems to me that the need opens the door to the little boy, but the little boy opens the door to the imagination. Because the little child is a crucial figure in the romantic imagination in Wordsworth, Blake, Rousseau. And this little child is where we'll speak of things beyond 'I need a lover.' Because if you go on with that little child, he will elaborate fantasy. He'll imagine, where do you want to be with your lover? And there'll be a scene. What will your father, who you want to find so much, say to you? And there'll be imagination. The little child isn't trapped only in the need, but he's a door to imagination. From the therapeutic view of the child as damaged, abused, molested, and so on, you move to the romantic view of the child as that part that has fallen, and cries out simply by being on earth. What it's longing for is something much more, it's huge.

In a book called *Biographies of Great People*, they tell the story of Stefansson, the polar explorer, and Manolete, the bullfighter. When they were small boys, they were both fearful. Stefansson used to stay home, he used to sail boats in the bathtub, he didn't mix with other kids. Manolete hung around his mother all the time, and at the age of nine, he actually sort of hung on her apron strings, or around the house. He was very afraid, a very timid little boy. Yet Manolete became one of the greatest bullfighters who ever lived.

Now, according to psychotherapy, of course, he became a bullfighter and Stefansson went to the North Pole because they were compensating for their childhood weakness. These were compensations, masculine protests. They became heroes because they were so mother-bound and soft as children.

But suppose you read the whole story *backward*. Suppose Manolete had the seed of being a great bullfighter within him and he knew that, and that was his acorn. What else would you do as a nine-year-old boy but hang around your mother, if you knew you had to meet a thousand-pound black bull with its horns out?

We read life only one way, and that's the dogma of psychology, which is called developmental psychology. But other cultures read life the other way—from the end, backward. The acorn is there, and the whole oak tree is in the acorn. The whole pattern is given in the Blake story, already given up there. And you choose the parents, according to the Platonic view, that are needed for your particular kind of tree. You can only be born in that family because that's the only place that would be right for your destiny. And the longer you spend protesting what your father and mother did to you, the more you're protesting that whole descent scenario.

The Manolete story is enormously important, to re-read your life backwards or all of a piece. It gives you another way of reading your weakness, why you 'couldn't' when you were little. But [psycho]therapy will keep you in that 'couldn't,' trying to work it through. The mother here is an obstacle. When I say the mother, you can talk about the outer mother, the inner mother or any 'mother.' An obstacle because the feeling that comes with the need then is, 'Please help me, I can't. I can't do this.' And the mother takes sympathy with this. 'Please love me, I'm so unloved. Please give me some softness. Please help me find my way. Please tell me my purpose.' And the mother will come in and do those things for you.

That raises the whole question of purpose that we've been talking about. Can someone else give you your purpose? Now, I don't think that's your question. I think your question is, 'How do I find my purpose?' And I'm suggesting that it's possible to find the purpose starting in the need, in the imagination of the child. In the fact that that child doesn't want to simply complain. And that his complaint is archetypal.[4] It starts off on the human level with a complaint such as 'I need love,' but what he wants is a divine fulfilment in love.

It's Blakean. The child's complaint is not merely a human complaint; there's something more in it, and that's divine fulfilment. The child is connected still to something beyond this world. And the intensity of its needs reflects the immensity of the world beyond from which it comes. So, if we're really doing developmental psychology, then we take the child all the way back beyond the birth passage, into the other world, into the Blakean world. And 'the child is father of the man.'

GRIEF AND DEPRESSION

ROBERT BLY I want you to hear a little poem by Antonio Machado:

> Mankind owns four things
> that are no good at sea:
> rudder, anchor, oars,
> and the fear of going down.

TIM WILSON To be 'at sea,' this suggests, is to be in a state of depression. We're tossed about on an ocean of feeling so deep that the rudder and oars we use for normal navigation are useless. Far better to fling ourselves overboard, dive willingly into the depths of grief.

ROBERT BLY There's a difference between grief and depression. Depression is where you feel vulnerable and helpless, and you feel how much has been lost in your life. There's no purpose in it, no passion in it. You can say it's passive, it belongs in the victim area. Somebody did it to me. You're angry at things that have happened to you, but who did it and exactly what they did is not brought to the surface. The experience is relatively unpleasant, and it doesn't encourage you to go down. In fact there's a whole bunch of uppers so that people don't go down.

Implied in all of our lives is a refusal to go down into masculine grief. You can say that in depression a hand comes up from

underneath and pulls you down. Because you gotta be down. That's the way it is on this planet. You gotta be down somewhere, sometime. And if you don't choose it, the hand up out of it will choose it. And then you don't know when you're gonna get out.

I fall into a depression and I have the sense this is the way it's going to be until the end of my life. You know, 'I don't want my friends to see me because everything I say is dull and boring.' So you start to separate yourself out. All your body processes slow down, you lose your eros completely, and your libido. And then all of a sudden one morning it's gone. Bam. That is so weird.

But grief is a different process. Grief has activity in it, in which you use the energy that men have had as hunters for thousands of years, and instead of going out to that world and hunting out there, you go down and hunt inside your childhood and various places.

When you make that distinction clearly, and stop being so passive, then you go down yourself, and you'll find it a nourishing experience.

The earliest statue found of a male god was in Romania. It's a beautiful little black basalt figure which appears with the figure of the Great Mother. Marija Gimbutas in her book *Goddesses and Gods of Old Europe* calls it the Sorrowful Male. It's bent over, and beautiful. Not depressed, but sorrowing. The strange implication is that the only power males have that is as strong as the Great Mother is their ability to descend in grief.

TIM WILSON But what are we grieving for? For many of us the feeling is present and poignant enough, but it seems to have no clear content or object. What have we men lost? For Wordsworth (and for Plato) it's the clouds of glory we trail. The grief in men began, says Bly, when our fathers left home at the time of the Industrial Revolution. And it's to industrial images he turns now, concrete images of failures in the form of man-made machinery, corroding at the bottom of Mother Ocean.

ROBERT BLY   Here's a poem I've been working on:

My father and I swim a mile or two apart
in a cold sea, aware of each other's
strokes. Both of us swim on, far from the
care of women. I go on asking my
shoulders why my lower half is so heavy.
Only my arms lift, the ocean pulls the
rest of me down. Far below us, there are
old model A engines, steel wheels from
rakes, engine blocks broken apart, drive
shafts sticking out of sand, the cutter bar
bent, smashed, pulleys from threshing
machines, scattered on the ocean floor.
Our failures lie solidified there, rusting,
in saline water.

We worked all day through dusk 'til
midnight and couldn't get it done.
Nothing helps. Drove a piston through
the block, it won't do. And so behind us,
a large beast follows, four or five miles
back, spines on his nose, fins like the
Komodo dragon, spiny whiskers,
following us.

TIM WILSON   The Wild Man would honour Mother Ocean and take nourishment from her, secure in his masculine heart, independent of any machines. But, out of touch with that, the wildness in Bly and his father becomes a gnarled, lumbering monster following behind, stalking them. In the meantime, thinking that they are 'far from the care of women,' they are swimming in the primordial Mother of life itself, dragging behind them the lower halves of their bodies where the source of their male energy has become atrophied and paralyzed. Here is reason for grief.

We have failed, then. But our gods have also fallen, and in our own time there are few men who seem to call out the best in us.

ROBERT BLY   Take a guru like Rajneesh. He has this material from India and he himself is a very intelligent person, a man of goodwill in general, I think. But what American males come to him with is their passivity. They're already in the state Blake calls Ulro, [of isolation, reflection, and jealousy]. All of them. And instead of asking them for creativity, he asks them to buy him a group of Cadillacs and Rolls-Royces. And they do it, you know, those American males, they do it. Then they wait by the roadside for him to drive by. But Blake is not in that area. Blake says, 'Either make your own system or be enslaved by another man's.'

Now the ladder of the guru, of total obedience and passivity, could be genetic with the Indians. It could be something independent inside of them developed by thousands of years of spiritual work. What if it doesn't hold for us? Have you ever read Norwegian and Swedish mythology? I don't see anything there about that. There's just big dragons all the time. You kill them 'til you're exhausted.

For myself, I find more spiritual energy in reading *Beowulf*. You get the picture of the monster Grendel ('the creature of the shadows . . . deprived of joys'). And then his mother (Ravenous and gloomy . . . she-wolf of the dread waters'). You rip off Grendel's arm, Beowulf rips the whole thing off. I guess it's a little like what Christ did. You can't deal with it piecemeal. Something big has to happen. Then you follow the blood and you dive down and there's his mother. And do you use your sword? It just falls to pieces right away. Her acid is so strong it dissolves your sword. You feel it smoke.

So you need a strong power from up in the spiritual and father realm in order to have guts enough to dive down into the water and meet Grendel's mother. We get on our scuba-diving stuff and go down five feet and look for the little, bright fish. It's really not the same.

TIM WILSON How, then, do we find passion and purpose in a godless world? One way, Bly says, is through the Logos, a principle which entered human consciousness to displace the Great Mother.[5] You can think of it as a sword that works—a sharp, discriminating, separating mode of thinking that has a masculine tone. Which is not to say that women don't have it as well.

Running amok with such a sword, it could be argued, is what

has led us to catastrophes, ecological and otherwise. But differentiating ourselves from the instinctual realm is one thing, and alienating is quite another.

Logos, then, is one way to passion for men. The other way is through Eros. And Eros loves the Wild Man.

EROS AND SEX TALK

ROBERT BLY   To me, the image I like best for Eros is that humming in the beehive that keeps the whole thing together. Eros is not abstract, it's a humming you can feel in your body. It takes all the parts of your body and it brings them together. It's like a glue, and physicists are looking now for the glue that holds the whole universe together. Sometimes after you make love, there'll be that kind of humming, and in a way your arms finally feel connected to your body. And your legs feel connected, and your heart feels connected.

I remember the first time I made love, I felt my soul come right down into my body afterward. And that was a joining, wasn't it? Where had it been before that time? I don't know. But that was Eros that brought it down into the body and I could then be with it. So I learned at that moment that you must never make love only once, because making love the first time is just to call your soul down, and to get rid of some sperm—we've got too much, anyway. And then, be sure to wait.

At this point the personality and character of the woman is

important, so that she is quiet and calm and not jumping up to play tennis or something like that. So that she wants you to be there, and you've got brains enough to stay there. Then you wait a little while, and the second lovemaking is the one she was really asking for the first time, because your soul will be in it this time. The third time even better: two souls in it then. Women are really tired of being made love to by men whose souls are up around the moon somewhere, isn't this so?

JAMES HILLMAN Now what I'm going to do is go right into the passion by applying Logos to Eros. So this is sex talk, and the main point is that male bonding requires sex talk. Men have to talk sex with each other, and men don't talk sex with each other, they talk sex with their women. When it's between men, it's often macho talk about what they could do or did do. They don't talk about details: what they like, what they want, what they get off on.

Usually with sex talk there's fear; it's a kind of counterphobia left over from adolescence. That is, we tell jokes, or we brag, or we boast. Sex as a victory, a conquest or an achievement. The bragging boy, dirty jokes.

But do we tell other men tales of impotence, the time when it didn't work, or the fear of inadequacy? Of being too small, too slow or too quick? Do we talk about that with another man? Do we have to go to a therapist to talk about it? Do we talk about our attraction to men's bodies, to the beauty of another man? Do we say to another man, 'You're beautiful to look at?' We'd never say that, unless we turn, come out of the closet and move to the other side of the line, but I'm talking now about heterosexual males. Do we admit the beauty of another cock, or the beauty of cock, and speak about that? Or talk about strange kinds of sex, of porn, of porn fantasies? We might sit next to another man and look at a porn movie, or have a gang party or something, but there won't be talk about it. Talk that has to do with intimacy. With feeling, the erotic aspect, the feeling aspect of sex.

Yet all of this we might do with a woman. Now do you see why we are therefore much more bound to women than we are to men? Because this most intimate part of our life we'll talk about with a woman, in detail. What we like, where we want to be touched, how we want to be touched, what fantasies we have, what we want to do, and so on, which we don't do with a man.

Part of the problem of talking with each other is that our language is bad. All the words we have for sex are macho words— cock, prick, dick, nuts, balls, suck, jerk, blow, yank. They're all good four-letter words. E.B. White would like those words. They're good, short Protestant nouns.

So the moment you begin to talk sex with another man, you find yourself caught in a language that is macho. We don't talk about 'jade stalks,' and 'opening lotuses,' and 'honey dew,' we say 'jism,' another four-letter word, and so on. We're paralyzed in our sexual imagination.

The sexual imagination is enormously important, and it is the turn-on. Yes, supposedly a nice ass is the turn-on, or skin, or hair, but language is also a turn-on. In the upper-class brothel that the British cabinet minister John Profumo went to, the job of one of the girls was to whisper in his ear, and describe what was happening while they were doing it. 'Doing it'— there you go. See how we tend to describe sex?

You remember the bowler hat that Sabina, the mistress in Kundera's *The Unbearable Lightness of Being*, wore? It was the thing that most attracted Tomàs. Well, that hat is the symbol of her sexual imagination.

And in Majorca, when a young woman was to be courted, to pick her husband, she would meet her suitors first. (This was supposedly in the last century. But it doesn't matter whether these things are true; we're not in the realm of science. We're in the realm of stories.) She would entertain the different prospective bridegrooms. They'd sit in an alcove, there'd be a chaperone in the room, they would whisper or talk very quietly, and he would tell her all the things he wanted to do with her. And she would pick her husband based on *his* erotic fantasies.

TIM WILSON The woman is shrewd enough to measure character in terms of imagination; the man courageous enough to express it. *Knowing what we want*, then, and not just when it comes to sex, is vital. Even more vital is putting it into words—an act, Bly reminds us, that too few of our fathers performed before their dragons caught up with them.

Blake might have saved them. And his counsel from 'Proverbs

of Hell' sounds more than just mischievous now: 'Sooner murder an infant in its cradle than nurse unacted desires.' Better, in other words, that the child should die than that he grow up with his Wild Man (remember the 'fiend'?) locked in the nursery.

So this is where we are: no longer in a nursery, quiet, and not just whispering in an alcove. We're drumming our hearts out with our brothers, here in the woods, to get up our courage. Courage for the leap we're about to make, yelling, newborn, into the world.   ◎

[1] 'The Age of the Wounded Male' by Robert Collison. *Saturday Night*, January/February 1979.

[2] 'Infant Sorrow' from Blake's *Songs of Innocence and of Experience*, London, Oxford University Press, 1970.

[3] 'To Tirzah' from *Songs of Innocence and of Experience*, London, Oxford University Press, 1970.

[4] Carl Jung coined the term 'archetype' to refer to ageless, recurrent patterns of human behaviour or experience.

[5] See 'Return of the Goddess' in *The Journal Of Wild Culture*, Vol. 1, No. 3.

ROBERT BLY is one of America's most influential poets. He followed his first prose work, *A Little Book on the Human Shadow* (New York: Harper and Row, 1988), with a hugely popular commentary on the Grimm fairy tale of the Wild Man, *Iron John*.

JAMES HILLMAN is author of *Re-Visioning Psychology* (New York: Harper and Row, 1975) and has written widely on the archetype of the *puer aeternus* (the eternal boy). He is one of the leading voices of renewal in the psychoanalytic tradition of Carl Jung.

For information about the annual men's event mentioned in this article, contact *The Minnesota Men's Conference, P.O. Box 4372, St. Paul, MN 55104.*

LET'S TALK

Words & Music by Paul Dutton © Transcribed and copied by Richard Maslove

WHITNEY SMITH

Togas, Codpieces, Corsets, and Bloomers:

THE PSYCHOLOGY
OF FASHION

CATHY DASEY

TAKE AS A STARTING POINT Oscar Wilde's observation: 'It is only shallow people who do not judge by appearances. The true mystery of the world is the visible, not the invisible.' Fashion, of course, is the art of the visible, the creation of an image of self instantly projected, read, and interpreted, obviously a far more sophisticated, controversial, sudden, and expressive business than the mere habit of wearing clothes and the history of costume might imply. We clothe our beliefs, prejudices, and dreams, our neuroses, our egos, and our id. Fashion is meaning, encoded in texture, colour, and style.

Much ink has been spent on the capriciousness of fashion, its relentless pursuit of the new and transient, its essential 'unnaturalness'—as though there were a correct, single understanding of natural man and woman we could all agree upon.

Fashion's artificiality is creative, interpretive, dangerous, perverse, political, sexist—all too human, ever present, and therefore 'natural,' if you like.

As the account in Genesis says quite specifically, along with their bad reputation, Adam and Eve acquired their first set of clothes. But it was Eve who bore the primary guilt ever after because it was Eve who was seduced by the snake, and it was she who, in turn, seduced Adam. Out of lust and shame came the clarion call for modesty and propriety, one of the oldest theories going for the origin and purpose of clothing. As for woman, she fell victim to man's imagination, a pattern that would dog her for centuries to come.

GLORIA STEINEM Male fantasy really focussed on Marilyn Monroe as somebody who would deliver infinite sexual pleasure with no demands whatsoever. She felt that she had to please men in order to be visible and have an identity, and looking like that was how Marilyn became visible; this meant bleaching her hair every week and worrying very much about the roots of her hair— and actually bleaching her pubic hair because she was once in an operating room and she felt that she had to live up to her public's expectations. She had plastic surgery of various minor sorts in order to narrow her nose and fix her jaw, and she wore extremely tight clothes and very wobbly high heels, creating the famous walk that we remember. It really strikes you when you look at photographs of her when she was younger, because here is this young woman, cheerful and healthy, with light-brown hair, who is actually an athlete. Later, Marilyn turned into a kind of female impersonator.

I think that there's a useful distinction to be made between fashion and style: fashion feels to me, as a word, like being told to dress a certain way; style feels to me like an individual thing—you find your own style. And why not? Why shouldn't we express ourselves with how we look? It isn't that one doesn't want to be sexual or sensual or show one's body. It has to do with whether the power is equal or not.

[1] Head of the History of Dress Department at the Cortauld Institute, University of London.

MARILYN POWELL   Over twenty years after her death, the image of Marilyn Monroe continues to haunt us. Her kind of innocence—if not purity—is a desire to please and to attract, and to be loved at all costs—qualities laid down long ago. But not all of my examples will be so blatant and primitive, clearcut in their distinctions of roles. The truth is, in life, as opposed to on screen, male and female roles have often been mixed; first one, then the other, obsessed with appearance and sex. And only the moralists have been able to keep them apart.

AILEEN RIBEIRO[1]   If you actually look at the medieval period, for example, the 14th century—when fashion as we know it can be said to begin, in the sense of fairly regular changes in cut and construction of clothing—women really are fairly modest in terms of their clothing. It is the men who excite the wrath of the moralist because they're the ones who are wearing short, immensely tight hose, so that the shape of their genitals is clearly shown. And priests are always sort of saying to people, 'Don't bend over, you know, because everything will be revealed.' So, from the end of the 15th century, right through into the first half of the 16th century, with regard to the codpiece, it really becomes a sort of integral part of masculine clothing, very much an element of masculine virility. I suppose if one had to pick out any fashion in the whole history of costume, the 16th century for men was the most flamboyant, the most ambitious, flaunting, and vaunting. There it all is, and—if you wanted to think of an example of overweening pride personified—there is your young man: perfumed, with an earring in one ear, sort of made up, with this immense codpiece, tightfitted doublet with a tiny waist, which he laces himself into with whalebone so that his waist is as tiny as a woman's. The fop, the gallant, the beau.

EDWARD MAEDER[2]   We are all prisoners of the time in which we live. For example, any of the nude studies that were done of Eve in the 15th century in the Lowlands, Dutch primitive paintings, they all have little, tiny round breasts that are very high, and they are very pear-shaped, which is a term that we use. That's

[2] Curator of Costume, the Los Angeles County Museum of Art.

exactly the figure that is emphasized by the clothing of the time, and, although artists did take certain liberties, you do see the stamp of the time.

Women in the late Middle Ages stood in something that we call the Gothic slouch, where the pelvis was jutted forward and the shoulders were pulled into the body slightly, and they would push along in front of them two feet of excess material on the end of their dresses. This was considered very graceful and very elegant.

With the Renaissance, there seemed to be a kind of resurgence of a more natural form for the bosom. It began to show up certainly in Venice in the 16th century. You saw a lot of what we now call goddesses, which were, of course, courtesans of the time, with everything, shall we say, hanging out.

It's something that has gone on for hundreds and hundreds of years, and that is that fashion sort of takes over and trains people to see things in a certain way. For example, because men wore knee-breeches, the calves were of course very obvious. And so these Downy Calves, which were developed in the 1780s, actually had pads woven into the calf part of the stocking, and it was a kind of male falsie, as it were. The aesthetic in each period is established through a series of circumstances that really aren't very clearly understood, and what fashion becomes is everyone's attempt to adapt to this stylish stance, or way of movement, or position of the bosom. We've pushed and pulled and shoved and padded. Now, of course, plastic surgery has come to our aid. But I should say virtually no one has ever had their breasts where they really belong, according to the aesthetic of the time. In 1900, for example, women wore their breasts in a form called the 'monobosom,' which really looked like one large bosom hanging down over the front of your belt. Well, that was to compensate for the S-shaped curve of the body. The way the woman was standing is that the buttocks were jutted backward so that this balanced this entire composition. It looks to us now to be totally absurd; but in 1900 it was considered simply beautiful.

[From *The Old Chevalier* by Isak Dinesen]
　　'Out of a tremendous froth of trains, pleatings, lace, and
　　flounces, which waved and undulated at every movement
　　of the bearer, the waist would shoot up like the chalice of

a flower, carrying the bust high and rounded as a rose, but imprisoned in whalebone up to the shoulder. Imagine now how different life must have appeared and felt to creatures living in those tight corsets, within which they could just manage to breathe, and in those fathoms of clothes that they dragged along with them wherever they walked or sat, and who never dreamed that it could be otherwise. A woman then was a work of art, the product of centuries of civilization, and you talked of her figure as you talked of her salon, with the admiration that one gives to the achievement of a skilled and untiring artist. And, underneath all this, Eve herself breathed and moved, to be indeed a revelation to us every time she stepped out of her disguise, with her waist still delicately marked by stays, as with a girdle of rose petals.'

MARILYN POWELL There is just a touch of cruelty about this spectacle of the rose—the woman with indentations in her flesh exposed to view. And notice something else. By the end of the 19th century, she stands alone. For centuries, female and male have vied equally for each other's attention. Now, Adam is an onlooker, frightened away perhaps by the accusation of the moralists about his own preoccupation with dress, that he's feminine if he overdoes it. And so Eve is busy turning into a clothes horse. What she carries with her out of her long involvement with the opposite sex is armour—padding on her hips and buttocks, whalebone encircling her waist. Even her breasts have been reshaped into a tantalizing illusion. It's not surprising that her disarray became a consummation to be wished for when everything else was foreplay and defence.

AILEEN RIBEIRO It is quite extraordinary that there is this immense divergence between very sober clothing for men—which of course goes on in infinite dreariness throughout the 19th century, getting darker and darker—and the very different clothing that is worn by the women in the 19th century. It's interesting because it seems to me that it is the first time in which you get two different aesthetics going on with regard to masculine clothing and feminine clothing. I think it was Quentin Bell who said that women are saying, 'I'm a little butterfly; I'm innocent; I really know nothing about the world; I am a kept woman'—in the literal sense of it. This is quintessentially very, very feminine, or making a statement about being feminine. And whether it's as a reaction to this, whether the women's reform movement would have indeed happened if it hadn't been as a reaction against this almost hot-house femininity, this almost overpowering sweetness that you get in the 19th century, I don't know. It's one of the big 'ifs' of the history of fashion and the history of society, that we really don't know.

MARILYN POWELL Ah, at last, some opposition to the fact that women were rendering themselves ridiculous, throwing practicality to the winds. From the women themselves, because there *was* opposition, right around the time Charles Frederick Worth was trying to establish himself as an arbiter in Paris of what they desired most. In Seneca Falls, New York, in the 1850s, a modest dress reform movement got underway. Among the reformers were Lucy Stone, Amelia Bloomer, Elizabeth Cady Stanton, and Susan B. Anthony. The women cut their skirts to the knees and put on ankle-length pantaloons underneath—trousers in effect. It was called the Bloomer costume. Traditionally, the skirt has symbolized female submissiveness. Historically, trousers have signified male power—power that was not yielded up easily to women.

SUSAN BROWNMILLER[3] The Bloomer campaign is certainly one of the more poignant moments in feminist history. Elizabeth Cady Stanton first, and her cousin, Susan B. Anthony, and of course Amelia Bloomer herself, all thought, 'Wouldn't it be wonderful if we could get out of these long skirts and corsets and wear something much more sensible?' In the language of the day, they called it the 'bifurcated dress.' Some variation on pants was what it was, and the cry went up that these women wanted to be men. They persevered for about seven years, but they had to give it up. And the fact that they failed so utterly and so miserably seems to tell us that you can call for things like the vote a lot more easily than you can call for changes in dress. So, here comes the women's movement, and we naturally look on dress and say, 'Well, how is this impeding our forward progress?' Certainly when

[3] Feminist and author of *Femininity*.

women were forced to wear corsets and hobbling skirts, hobbling shoes, it's quite clear that fashion was something negative in terms of women's rights and women's progress.

The issue for me is not simply pants versus skirts. I think I would probably object far less if there were equality there. But, you know, men are still in charge in society, and women are not.

MARILYN POWELL   Did we return to the pressure for women to wear skirts?

SUSAN BROWNMILLER   I see women were far more reluctant to wear pants in the '80s than they were in the '70s, particularly career women. It's as if you can't let your ambition show in too many places at once, and, if you're determined to be successful, you'd better look conventional.

MARILYN POWELL   Does it mean, do you think, that the women's movement has receded?

GRANT McCRACKEN[4]   It's fascinating to read 19th-century literature and to see what the suffragettes were up against. Male commentators were saying that there could be no doubt that women ought not to vote, and that the most striking proof one could have of this argument was the change of bonnets every season. Men had succeeded in persuading women to enter a gilded cage. Then they could say, 'Look at women; look how they dress; they deserve the subordinate status they have.' And that's what gave real energy, I think, to the suffragette attempt to change the style of female dress. But a development takes place in the 20th century to claim another symbolism. I've looked at John Molloy's book, *Dress for Success,* in which he suggests that women have to strike a balance between dressing for success and dressing in a manner that appears positively to invite sexist treatment in the workplace, for instance, either in the form of sexual invitation or managerial arrogance. Molloy argues that women were victims of those attitudes because their clothing seemed almost to reinforce their subordinate status in the world of work. What one has to do to change this is indeed to borrow the properties of male clothing in which authority has been encoded, but not to go too far. He

[4] Anthropologist from the University of Guelph, Ontario.

says it's absolutely crucial to make this transition without reproducing the clothing of men.

MARILYN POWELL *The Woman's Dress for Success Book* by John Molloy appeared in 1977, by the time women were firmly established in the workplace. It was enormously successful. The evidence was everywhere: gone were the frilly blouses and Peter Pan collars, styles that hinted at dependence and whimsicality. In came tailored suits, shirts and ties, even jockey shorts for 'her.'

GRANT McCRACKEN Industrial capitalism demands a kind of domestication of the individual, a willingness to subordinate one's individuality to the demands of the workplace. There's an odd tension between two ideas: one, that the individual is supposed to suppress certain aspects of the self in order to be a successful part of the industrial system; and two, the ideal of individual expression, also a part of that system. In any case, there's something about the business suit that represents a kind of deliberate shutting down of the self for certain purposes. That is what women quite properly have identified as the most irksome aspect of the dress-for-success movement of the last ten years; it has asked them to participate in the shutting down of the self in order to properly honour the demands of the world of work. Dress-for-success, image management, the demonstration of prestige through their wardrobe . . . We're fickle; we may criticize them, but we expect people in power to dress their part.

Lately, we've been in an elitist phase, if we're to judge by the style of politicians and their wives. Brian Mulroney hides Gucci shoes in his closet. Raisa Gorbachev has been seen shopping at Cartier's, while Nancy Reagan buys at Bloomingdale's. And lately too, we've allowed our museums (of all places) to collude in their conspicuous consumption—by presenting fashion shows endorsing the cult of appearance and the connection between power and expensive clothes.

In 1981, a costume exhibition called 'The 18th-Century Woman, from 1690 to 1790' opened in New York at the Metropolitan Museum. There were 130 costumes, chiefly from France. The galleries were sprayed with French perfume, and the mannequins on which the magnificent costumes were displayed were painted gold or sheathed in metallic stockings. They were unreal, attenuated, high-fashion mannequins, usually seen in department store windows or fashion photographs, and the combination of 18th-century grand dressing and 20th-century chic was startling. 'The 18th-Century Woman' was only the first of the costume shows staged by Diana Vreeland, editor for 30 years of *Harper's Bazaar* and *Vogue* magazine, and now Special Consultant to the Costume Institute at the Metropolitan Museum. Vreeland's connections with the fashion industry and her promotion of their products, along with her reading of the past, have all come under attack in one book. *Selling Culture: Bloomingdale's, Diana Vreeland, and the New Aristocracy of Taste in Reagan's America* is by historian Debora Silverman. Here Silverman singles out the show on the 18th-century woman.

DEBORA SILVERMAN What Vreeland did, which was typical of her exhibitions, was put together the show as if it were a fashion show. Daywear, summer wear—she looked only at the surface of the images, and particularly at the luxury on the surface of those images. But, of the culture out of which they came, this defied meaning, value, and function. In the show, she identified the 18th century as a century of female independence and power. What she meant by this is not what we might think of; that is, the enlightened salons of intellectual women, which certainly were there. She identified aristocratic women for the way they seduced men in power to do their bidding. So, it's the image of the woman using her sexuality to gain power, which is the old model of a certain form of female power through physical appearance.

Americans are always inventing their own history, and the American rich are always looking to Europe and elsewhere to find a tradition through culture. But it was a very peculiar exclusion, Vreeland's interest in the 18th century as a century, as she called it, 'of dreaming and opportunity and exaltation, close to the way we live today.' She showed many costumes of aristocratic women, one of whom went to the guillotine. The fact is, the tremendously glaring and emphatic statements of wealth were made in the 18th century amidst the greatest depravation society had seen in many, many years. The costumes show that what Vreeland celebrated were spectacles of wealthy people from the past as if they were aristocracies with privilege without responsibility, which is very different from how aristocracies were defined and operated. There was a system of privilege with responsibility, whether it was lived out or not. 'There is no poverty here,' as she said, 'there is only luxury and snobbism.' So the shows really were images of the good life.

MARILYN POWELL Museums traditionally have preserved the best-made and most artistic, which largely has amounted to the possessions of the wealthy. But hitherto such institutions have not endorsed a certain lifestyle, even implicitly. It comes down to our deciding what we want the history of our material culture to reflect. Out on the streets of New York City these days, another kind of history is being evoked and a different kind of demonstration of the power of dress is being made, as Stuart Ewen of the Media Studies Program at Hunter College points out.

STUART EWEN There is something eerie about walking the streets of New York. In a society where the conception of prosperity is so much rooted in a symbolic economy—a paper economy—certain elements of the society can wear more and more mink while large numbers of people are out there homeless. Even to think about 'the Yuppie' as the archetype of American society means that the images of prosperity have overwhelmed the reality of social experience.

You know, hierarchy isn't just an observation that somebody might make about society in the past. Hierarchy was visually made legible, and there were a lot of ways in which sovereigns and people at the top of society made their power legible to the general population: the use of materials, for example, certain rare silks, velvets, ermine. A thousand yards of cloth would be used to produce a single garment. Well, that's a very visible statement to make: that what it takes to clothe me is the equivalent of what it would take to clothe an entire village of commoners. I think there has been the reinstitution of this idea of visible, legible privilege as an element within our society. Again, in the 20th century, there is a battle between a conception of poverty as something that can be ameliorated and that justice should ameliorate, and a more conservative and elitist perspective, that essentially views poverty as the result of laziness, of moral bankruptcy. And not only is clothing a mark of how much money you make; built into that is the assumption that what somebody wears makes who they are.

DEBORA SILVERMAN   You can see across the culture, in advertising, in fashion, in magazines, this whole emphasis on 'the good life,' the insulated good life, the appeal to distinction, aristocracy. For instance, in images of high style, from advertisements such as 'Living a Cutty above' for Cutty Sark, to *Vanity Fair*, which has a kind of obsession with royalty and with cultural figures as new forms of nobility. There is a certain voyeurism in 'Lifestyles of the Rich and Famous,' in 'Dynasty,' which brings politicians such as Ford and Kissinger on the show. At the same time, there is a very big fashion push for *haute couture*, the appeal to aristocratic lineage and tradition in the wide manufacture of fashion and how we look today. There is a very deep correspondence between this culture of opulence and the kind of politics of greed and attitude toward wealth that the Reagans, fo example, encouraged. Not that the Reagans established the context, but underlying it is the notion that there is no sacrifice nor process nor social responsibility. This is a tremendous statement of disdain for not only history and the past, but a disdain for the social others. The exaggerated tendencies of the early Reagan years have been tempered. But the wider cultural resonance of the permission to 'live well and have the best revenge,' as these people call it, is to be involved in self-display and to repudiate any form of responsibility for social others. *Get rich*—that is the main message today. And it's something that's very disturbing.

Call it glamour, style, power, distinction, or flair—shape the fantasy as you will—you can't consider fashion without confronting the lure of fame. It's the look of high fashion that makes celebrities out of models, our ticket to a world that's flawless, where we are all voyeurs. It's the Hollywood dream machine in which movie stars are fabricated out of mainstream America, with the suggestion that their look in every way could become our own. It's public relations, the teen-age dress code, performance, rebellion, and fancy dress, and what it comes down to is recognition in the eyes of others. The world as our looking glass.

It was artist Andy Warhol who said that we're constantly seeking acceptance. No. Actually he said: 'In the future, everyone will be famous for fifteen minutes.' That is our fantasy, at any rate. Gael Love is editor of *Interview*, the magazine in New York that Warhol founded in 1969.

GAEL LOVE   There was a great line in *The Big Chill* when the Glenn Close character says, 'Oh, you know, I hate to think that everything we did in the '60s was just fashion'. But, in a way, everything that we all do in every way is just fashion. At the magazine, we put it into movie star category. You have politician-as-movie-star; you have sports-figure-as-movie-star. Everybody wants to be famous. I heard somebody from a think tank a little while ago saying that, by the year 1990, one out of ten people would have been on TV in the world, if only for a couple of seconds in a crowd scene. And I think that, because people read about celebrities all the time, they want a piece of that pie for themselves. Last year, we did a Hollywood issue. The first twenty pages were all new kids. When I was telling people about it, I said, 'Take a good look at these kids because you may never see them again.' I mean, they're having their moment. For instance, Andy's quote—I think that Robert Hughes in *Time* said it has taken on Orwellian proportions, the fact that literally everybody in all the different facets of life can be famous, but just for a little while. The magazines have done that through stylizing fame, packaging it, mass marketing it, and throwing it away.

KENNEDY FRASER[5]   The world of fashion has always been a very volatile and open sort of world, and there is a star quality that some people have. People don't necessarily have to have any particular social background—you know, in New York, you can become a part of the scene just because you want to be a part of it—you just have to keep showing up. There's been a tremendous amount of conspicuous consumption. A lot of people have made a lot of money very fast, and, for the first time in many years, recently, the wives of very rich men have become terribly much photographed, and their chief claim to fame is that they are the wives of wealthy men. Now we have two young women in the British royal family who, to some extent, are setting the tone, and people are looking to Princess Diana and Fergie for what they wear. But that has nothing to do with the fact that they're aristocrats because what they are is super-celebrities, media celebrities.

[5] Writer for *The New Yorker* and author of *Scenes from the Fashionable World*.

MARILYN POWELL   Are you saying to me that 'celebrity' takes the place of the word 'aristocrat'?

KENNEDY FRASER   I think it probably does, yes. The important thing is to be a celebrity.

MARILYN POWELL   What does it mean to be a celebrity?

KENNEDY FRASER   It means to be a packaged person. It means to be an image. I feel in many ways that we're living in a kind of Dark Ages. A small group of incredibly wealthy people in their castles are just spending untold amounts of money on conspicuous consumption. Of course, the Middle Ages were a great moment for spiritual life, the time when the great monastic orders were being founded, and in our time too we're going to see a great resurgence of spirituality.

WELL, ALL THE WORLD'S A STAGE, as Shakespeare observed, and each new context, each new age confers its own artifice. If dramatic allusion is an element in the presentation of self, we may well wonder what clothes we will design to body forth a new-age spirituality. Fashion can't save a culture or a city or a human life, but it continues to define us, revealing a psychology to ourselves, as individuals and in groups. Through the best and the worst of times. ◉

GALLERY

CHRIS NICHOLS

CHRIS NICHOLS

FILL IN THE BLANKS

*'Protecting our Environment: An Ongoing Commitment'—
a pre-Earth Day speech for chemical industry managers, distributed by
the Chemical Manufacturers Association (USA)*

APRIL 22 IS EARTH DAY, rather it is the 20th anniversary of Earth Day. Twenty years ago—in 1970—a head of steam was building up across the country. People—many of them young and outside the 'establishment'—were becoming concerned about the environment.

The Great Lakes were in trouble because of raw human waste and industrial pollutants (OR USE LOCAL EXAMPLE). Rivers had caught fire. And we were just beginning to understand the health risks to young children from lead poisoning.

Smokestacks were changing from being symbols of industrial might and progress to being the way to track down somebody who was polluting the air. There was also a feeling that business and government did not care about protecting the environment.

From all of this, a national movement was born. The purpose of this movement was to broaden the awareness of our need to protect and preserve our environment.

When April 22, 1970 rolled around, excitement was in the air. At the time, Earth Day was one of the largest mass participation events in U.S. history. Marches closed streets, and there were pickets at industrial facilities, and teach-ins at colleges and universities.

Some estimates put the number of people involved at 20 million. Most businesses at the time hoped that by ignoring Earth Day, it would disappear. Here in (LOCAL COMMUNITY), Earth Day was (LOOK IN ISSUES OF LOCAL NEWSPAPERS TO SEE IF IT WAS IGNORED, CELEBRATED, ETC., OR SHARE PERSONAL EXPERIENCE OF 20 YEARS AGO)

Since that first Earth Day 20 years ago, the environment has improved. That's due largely to the many federal and state laws we now have on air quality, clean water, managing waste, auto emissions, and land use. These laws didn't exist prior to 1970 and are clearly an outgrowth of Earth Day.

These laws are overseen by the Environmental Protection Agency—which celebrates its 20th birthday in December. In our state, the (NAME OF AGENCY) is responsible for protecting our natural surroundings.

Two decades later, rivers aren't catching on fire. The Great Lakes are fishable and swimmable, and their quality is improving all the time. According to EPA, we are making progress in the fight against air pollution.

• For example, the amount of lead in the air decreased 88% between 1978 and 1987, and fell 19% between 1986 and 1987.

• Carbon monoxide emissions—the stuff that comes out of your car's tailpipe—were down 32% between 1978 and 1987 and fell 6% between '86 and '87.

• Sulfur dioxide dropped 35%—3% from '86 to '87.

• Ozone dropped 16%—5% from '86 to '87.

• Nitrogen dioxide levels dropped 12% from '78 to '87, with no change reported from '86 to '87.

At our facility, we have also improved in the last 20 years. In 1970, we didn't have an environmental manager. Now we do, and (HE/SHE) has a staff of (X) people.

Twenty years ago, we didn't coordinate closely with the fire department in responding to incidents in our plant. Now we do. Two decades ago, we didn't do any testing or monitoring to see how far our emissions travelled. Now we do.

Since that first Earth Day, we have installed control equipment to reduce our releases to air, land and water.

It costs us (X) dollars a year to operate this equipment, but it's worth every cent because the equipment has cut our emissions by (X) percent over the past (X) years.

Nowadays, we handle waste by (X METHOD/PROCESS) as compared to (Y MEHOD/PROCESS) 20 years ago.

Besides doing all of these things, we have beautified our plant. IF APPROPRIATE, NAME OTHER SPECIFIC IMPROVEMENTS.

Is everything perfect? Absolutely not. Is there a need to do more? You bet. This year, we will be adding to our efforts to protect the environment. We will be installing _____. We will be monitoring _____. We will be spending _____ to operate pollution control equipment.

We will be (HOLDING AN OPEN HOUSE, SPONSORING A RECYCLING DAY, PLANTING TREES, CREATING AND MANAGING A PUBLIC ADVISORY PANEL).

Beyond all of those things, we pledge:

• To listen and respond to community concerns about chemicals and our operations.

• To develop and produce chemicals that can be manufactured, transported, used and disposed of safely.

• To make health, safety and environmental considerations a priority in our planning for existing and new products and processes.

• To report promptly to government officials, employees, customers and the public any information on chemical-related health or environmental hazards and to recommend protective measures.

• To operate our facility in a manner that protects the environment and the health and safety of our employees and the public.

• To work with others to resolve problems created by past handling and disposal of hazardous substances. And finally . . .

• To work with government officials in creating responsible laws, regulations and standards to safeguard the community, the workplace and the environment.

Simply put, my company and the plant I manage are committed to a continuing effort to improve our responsible management of chemicals.

Over the next _____ (ads will run the second and third weeks of April), you may see an advertisement in *Time* or *People* or *National Geographic*, or other magazines and newspapers about a new chemical industry initiative called Responsible Care: A Public Commitment.

One-hundred seventy-five of the nation's chemical companies that account for over 90% of industial chemical production in North America will be putting their names behind this ongoing effort to improve performance in health, safety and environmental quality. (NAME OF COMPANY) was one of the first signers of the pledge.

All of us have come a long way since that first Earth Day 20 years ago. 'They'—those environmental types—the tree huggers—are becoming all of us, our fellow workers, our collective future.

We can—and should—work together to ensure an environment that is clean and that meets our needs. Thank you!

WHAT GOES AROUND

A SIX-QUART BASKET of peaches, another of zucchini and new potatoes.

I set them down, side by side on the kitchen counter. They had been picked at the moment of perfect ripeness and looking at them gave me a thrill of pleasure. I reached my cookbook down and began thumbing through for a recipe that might combine all three. Crossing the room, I disturbed the cloud of fruit flies hovering over the compost bucket I had meant to empty before going out shopping. Food scraps rotted fast in this heat. Insects helped. When I kicked open the back door and carried the bucket out, the cloud followed like a genie chasing its bottle.

The *Country Echo* had reported a garbage crisis. Residents were being urged to participate in a recycling programme, so we all began bundling up our newspapers, glass and tin cans and dropping them off at the depot downtown, waiting to be alone and unobserved before pitching in our liquor bottles. The *Echo*'s how-to article on composting made it sound easy and inexpensive, so I bought the recommended plastic garbage pail, cut the bottom out, punched holes for ventilation below the lid and around the sides and planted it beside the flower bed.

What I'd begun out of civic obligation became intensely satisfying. Redirecting the river of squandered material flowing through my life freed me of tremendous guilt but it was heavy work. Like the human body, organic kitchen waste was about eighty per cent water. My accumulation of banana peels, bread crusts, egg shells, tea bags, pea hulls, cantaloupe rinds, and coffee grounds had to be aerated every few days with a pitchfork and tending my compost now displaced most of the other pleasures of my day. I became fanatical about not letting the smallest chip of vegetable matter escape into the regular garbage. These six-quart baskets sitting on my counter—zucchinis, peaches, new potatoes, small and freckled like eggs laid by the ground itself—were bright links in a chain of coexistence. Vegetables were on their way to two mouths—mine and the one hidden under the lid of the bin. Between us, every atom—and I was becoming more sensible of the molecular universe—would be put to good use, a Sprat-and-wife symbiosis.

My soul was nourished spiritually by such insights. Dining with other people, I found myself scrutinizing their plates, twitching to scrape whatever they left behind into a folded napkin, slip it into my pocket, feed it to my other mouth.

Occasionally, I lapsed back into old habits. My hand would mindlessly pitch a newspaper into the fireplace, rinse out the teapot under the tap, coming to with horror just as the swirl of leaves, excellent source of nitrogen, escaped down the drain. I paid penance for these lapses by meticulously collecting the wispy garlic papers and peppercorn hulls that had accumulated behind my stove and trans-porting them, pinch by reverent pinch, outside.

Reports were coming in from everywhere that global pollution was irreversibly advanced. Too little being done too late. The earth was doomed. I lay down on the lawn with the newspaper folded under my head and stared into the trees, waiting for something inside to pull me up again. Like continents that had once been attached, the armoured plates of my psyche were drifting apart while I lay passive as an ocean beneath them, powerless to nudge them back together.

The ground was damp.

I stood up and brushed the blades of grass off my legs back onto the lawn. I headed for the mall, a hearth drawing nigh new generations of shoppers in timeless pursuit of redundant supplies and the latest disposable products, herding their kids into gasoholic family wagons, lurching back onto the crowded highway to drive a few short yards home. I'd seen films of such placed speeded up, the head- and taillights gaily fusing into party streamers—and slow-mo photography too, which elevated the plainest of human gestures—the slap of a credit card onto the counter, the cashier's blink and spreading smile—to the eloquence of poetry.

I stood out behind Family Restaurant staring at the dumpster bins stocked full of leftover food, paper garbage and industrial-sized tins, buckets, and bottles that had held the fats, salts, sugars, alcohols, and blood the restaurant combusted into currency.

So much squandered possibility.

In the dying light, the dumpsters looked like giant six-quart baskets of organic, recyclable material—if only the restaurant could be persuaded to label them so and thus pre-sort its garbage, saving people down the road one horrible job and substantially reducing the burden of landfill on the municipality. If I could persuade Family Restaurant—a franchise—then perhaps Burger King might follow suit, and McDonald's. A chain reaction across North America, triggered by me.

I began to pace the lot, rehearsing how to pitch the concept to the manager—or perhaps I'd start with a letter to the Chamber of Commerce, confront those polyester opportunists responsible for putting this mall here in the first place or the merchants' association, goad it into taking the initiative. On the other hand, the same letter coming from a politician . . . who was my member of Parliament?

A pair of kitchen workers came staggered out to swing four more garbage bags overhand into the bin. The smell, punched loose by the impact, hit me in the throat and I had to retreat quite a distance. The asphalt around the bins was greasy and stained with spoilage. Liquid from dumpsters everywhere was trickling into the sewers, braiding into oily underground rivers that emptied eventually into the seas, to be taken up again as rain, pelted down into our open mouths, our waiting fields, drawn into the veins of our unborn children.

I covered my face with my hands.

I couldn't undertake the global consciousness-raising of restauranteurs and their patrons. I couldn't reclaim enough good earth from this ocean of refuse to make any difference whatsoever and anyway, why did I want to? I hated the process of decay and change. Every year, when the lake turned cool, the days shortened and dead leaves began to scratch across the sidewalks, I was seized with a melancholia so sharp and physical, its pangs felt almost sexual while the fragrant air of spring, the receding rags of snow reminded me only of lilies and death. Another year gone.

THE NEWSPAPERS continued to strafe with their statistics of despair.

I had started my compost bin in late summer. We had an early, sharp fall and everything froze solid on Hallowe'en. I checked the contents in December, but nothing much had changed. Summer's corncobs and broccoli trunks were still quite recognizable, even a clump of bean sprouts.

By March, I noticed that the contents had become less distinct, more compact, and by the end of May no matter how many buckets I emptied into it, the level always fell a little by the next day.

Whenever friends dropped by I showed them my bin, rolling it aside to reveal the muck percolating through. I wanted to convert them to my new pleasure, seduce them with my philosophy of decay—confiding that the transformative processes of death no longer dismayed me, that it was profoundly comforting to see that nothing truly disappeared—or therefore appeared—within this closed system, that I'd found support for the notion of reincarnation.

Some listened, others did not, preferring instead to stagger back theatrically clutching their noses. I explained that the telltale stink of anaerobia could be reduced by vigorous pitchforking and I was doing just that after a particularly wet week in July when I noticed masses of thin, red worms, a decompositional milestone. By now, my fork was turning over something that resembled dirt but was mucky enough to pull a boot off.

August 24th. Today, in triumph, I lifted the lid and pitched the contents onto the flower bed. The characteristic forms of all the fruits and vegetables I had thrown in for a year had been assimilated into a material indistinguishable from store-bought gardening soil. I picked up a handful, studied it, plucked out an errant elastic band, squeezed my hand shut. When I opened it again the earth held its shape like stiff dough. I spread the grains apart with my thumb, red-black crumbs, purple-black, some flecks of orange, but basically uniform in colour and free of seeds and insects.

Spread out on the palm of my hand was the elegant proof of ashes to ashes, dust to dust. We come out. We will go back in. We will be dissolved into one another. For ever and ever. Amen. ◉

RICK/SIMON

THE BEER CAN
OR THE HIGHWAY?

Ecology might lose its soul as it comes of age

IT WAS SUNDAY MORNING at 11 o'clock and David Suzuki was
on the radio, warning of the environmental catastrophe looming
around his listeners. A generation ago most of us would have been
in church at this time; and here we were in church again. Dr.
Suzuki's programme, with its visions of Armageddon and its call
to repentance and conversion, was surely a sermon. His text
imputed collective guilt to his audience, much as a church con-
gregation might be told that it was their sins for which their Lord
had died. 'We' were burning rainforests, boring holes in the ozone,
and washing topsoil away, and we must stop. In the old words of
the Anglican Book of Common Prayer, we had done those things
which we ought not to have done, and we had left undone those
things which we ought to have done, and there was no health in us.
This fairly familiar environmentalist dis-
course is essentially a mystification, particularly
in its eagerness to assign responsibility to an
undefined, undifferentiated 'us.' To me,

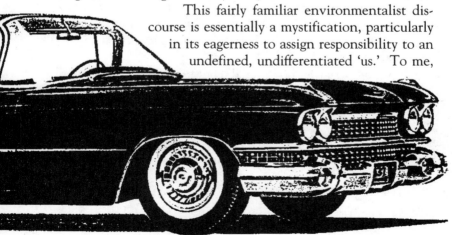

collective responsibility is, as Hegel says, a night in which all cows are black. It conflates the over-consuming rich with the under-consuming poor, those who direct production with those who only carry out their directives, and the conveniently enlightened corporate 'environmentalists' of the late 80s with those who have already lived the ecological gospel for nearly a generation. Worse, by lumping everyone into the economic category of 'consumers,' it overlooks the cultural dimension in which solutions are actually to be found. But on this particular Sunday, I saw something new in David Suzuki's repeated use of the 'we.'

Perhaps, I thought, it was not meant as a description of any existing entity. David Suzuki, after all, must know as well as I do, that except in a biological and behavioural sense, there really is no such thing as 'humanity' in general. Insofar as people have lived in different cultures and told different stories about who they are, they have lived in different times and spaces, and there has been no central privileged time in which a global 'we' could exist. Humanity as such has no past and, therefore, in the sense that two points are needed to make a line, no future. There is no collective subject that marches through a uniform, world-historical time polluting the waters and laying waste the lands. There are Canadians and Brazilians and Indonesians, each subdivided in turn by class, culture, gender, and ideology, acting out of specific historical circumstances. So I concluded that David Suzuki's 'we' must be an educational ploy, an attempt not to describe this imaginary collective subject of history, but to evoke it. As he reconstructs history in terms of ecology, this new planetary being, or species being, comes into view; and as he addresses it, he, in effect, calls it into being.

Understanding this, however, did not fill me with confidence. On the contrary, I fear that as ecology becomes the new religion, and the past is transformed into the prehistory of the age of ecology, there is a possibility that the dimensions of human experience that elude the science of ecology will be forgotten. The planetary 'we,' in other words, might obliterate history and homogenize culture.

It is a commonplace that the pictures of the Earth taken from space had a revolutionary impact on human consciousness. Seeing this blue globe with its delicate tracery of clouds and its green mantle of vegetation, it is said, made us aware that we are one planetary species, and that this finite blue ball is our precious and vulnerable home. But there is another side to this image. It generates an illusion that the Earth is something that one person can actually hold in mind and encourages people to think of the Earth as something that we can and should master and manage as 'our' planet. There is a temptation in this to megalomania, in which 'we' in effect become God.

Some of the ambiguity of the Whole Earth image can be understood by thinking about how the pictures were obtained in the first place. The space programme that produced them, after all, derives from the same technological will-to-power that has produced the environmental crisis. And this technological will-to-power, in turn, derives from a type of science that has gradually convinced people that an external, objective view of things is in some deep sense the only true view. Earth-seen-from-the-moon is the ultimate in objective distance from ourselves—beautiful yes, but still only a ball spinning alone in empty space. I should say here, lest you begin to think that I am writing as a member of the Flat Earth Society, that I'm not denying that this is part of what the Earth is. But it is not how we ourselves experience the Earth; it is not, phenomenally speaking, what the Earth is.

There is a story about the poet William Blake being at dinner with some people of a scientific turn of mind who were discoursing enthusiastically about the incredible distance between planets, the time light takes to reach the Earth, and so on. Blake listened with increasing agitation, and then finally burst out, 'Tis false. I was walking down a lane the other day, and at the end of it, I touched the sky with my stick.' In A Vision of the Last Judgment Blake wrote:

'What, 'it will be Question'd, when the sun rises do you not see a round disk of fire somewhat like a Guinea? 'O no, no, I see an Innumerable company of the Heavenly host crying, 'Holy, Holy, Holy is the Lord God Almighty.'

Blake opposed the ascendant science of his day not because he denied that in some limited sense it was true. It was simply 'single vision,' a way of seeing that disenfranchised the imagination and made the guinea sun more 'real' than the innumerable company of the heavenly host. The Whole Earth image is a kind of guinea sun: a technological construction of seductive beauty that claims a privileged place in our perception as the real world. It substitutes a bounded physical sphere of which we are implicitly lords for the Earth as an imaginative reality within which we are subjects. And it replaces the subjective experience of an Earth that extends inwards to infinity with an externalized objective globe.

These two views, of course, are not really alternatives to each other any longer and we have no real choice between them. With the finite objective planet at the threshold of disaster, there is no possibility of abandoning the science that shows it to us. But it would also be unwise not to devote the occasional moment to contemplating the fact that the science that claims to know the solution to the environmental crisis is also in the first place its cause. Without this saving insight the cure might turn out to be worse than the disease.

The problem of science is encoded in an interesting way in the very term ecology; for ecology is the banner of both science and anti-science. It describes, in the first place, a scientific discipline based on mathematics and on computer modelling, which traces energy flows through physical systems. But it is also the self-chosen designation for a protest movement, with its roots in European Romanticism and American Transcendentalism, which has been, above all, a critique of science as objectivity. In the heady atmosphere of 1970, at the time of the first Earth Day, it may have seemed to many that these two tendencies were finally reconciled; but this does not in retrospect seem to me to have happened. It looks rather as if 'environmentalism' has been the Trojan horse for a scientific and managerial ethos that is exactly the opposite of what the radicals of the movement intended. This ethos is captured in the claim of the United Nations' Brundtland Commission that the new planetary reality must not only be recognized but 'managed,' a claim repeated so often in recent years that it has come to seem an unremarkable cliché rather than a piece of extraordinary hubris. It is for this reason that the environmental movement has split into at least two distinct strands: those who want to focus the existing institutions of society on the problem of 'saving the environment,' and those who see in the environmental crisis both the necessity and the opportunity to overthrow those institutions. (There is little homogeneity on either side of this divide—the reformists argue about whether or not to endorse environmentally friendly groceries, and the radicals argue over whether deep ecology or social ecology is the true religion—but to me this division still dwarfs the differences within either camp.) The question at issue is whether economy is going to be overthrown as the ruling force in all our lives, or whether the stranglehold of economic assumptions is going to be strengthened by the addition of a whole new set of environmental constraints. One side wants to make the system more 'resource efficient,' the other to question the very idea that the world is composed of resources. One wants to save the environment, the other to suggest that by even speaking of an environment as something external to us, we already locate ourselves within the discourse that has estranged us from Nature in the first place.

It is now the case that a vast abstraction called The Economy rules our lives and defines what constitutes civic virtue. It is a long time since anybody pretended that production should be subjected to the decision of some human community as to whether that production was good or needful. Production is good in itself. The growing pollution and degradation of air, land, and water challenged this view. 'Environmentalism,' at first, was simply the realization that conservation of Nature absolutely contradicts the possibility of unending economic growth. But in recent years a new approach has been evident. It is symbolized by the many reports emanating from the offices of the Worldwatch Institute, the World Resources Institute, the Brundtland Commission, and the various agencies of the UN.

The Brundtland Commission, set up by the UN in the early 80s to study the relationship between environment and development, is typical in its call for environmental protection to be harmonized with economic development in 'a new era of growth.' The essence of this approach is the claim that economic development can be made sustainable simply by factoring the environment into economic decisions. In the capitals of industrialized countries, where environmentalists like Brian Mulroney and Margaret Thatcher rule, this translates into a vision of business as usual but with the added dimension of resource efficiency. Business may even improve. The Toronto *Globe and Mail* for July 31, 1989, reported, under the headline 'Anti-Pollution Backlash Sparks Boom Industry,' that in Ontario protecting the environment is a $2 billion industry comprising 1,800 companies and 28,000 jobs.

It is highly unlikely, in fact impossible, that this sunny vision of an ecological capitalism in which the world has its cake and eats it too, can succeed in the long term. But, in the short term, it can certainly cloud political issues and confuse political debate. Worse, the gospel of resource efficiency threatens to extend ecological self-consciousness into every aspect of daily life.

The late American novelist Edward Abbey was once entertaining an interviewer from some environmentally conscious magazine and as they drove down a highway near Abbey's Arizona home, Abbey threw a beer can out of the car window. The interviewer was visibly shocked—possibly Abbey's purpose—but Abbey explained that the beer can by itself was simply an interesting object, and possibly even quite diverting for the creatures who would subsequently chance across it. The problem, he concluded, was not the beer can but the highway.

When I first heard this story a few years ago, I identified more with the outraged interviewer than with the hairy-chested novelist who could throw beer cans out the window with impunity because he had the higher consciousness. Today I'm not so sure. The concern now being evoked by the environmental crisis seems to be so firmly fixed on the beer can, and so unaware that it is only the highway that makes the beer can a problem, that I'm more inclined to sympathize with Abbey. We may become a resource-efficient society that knows to recycle the beer can; but this still does not put in question the underlying assumption that the world is composed of potential economic inputs called resources. In fact it may strengthen the assumption.

The word 'environment' has become what the German scholar Uwe Poerkson calls a 'plastic word.' (To translate the German *Plastikwoerter*, Ivan Illich has proposed the evocative English equivalent 'amoeba words.') It stretches to fit every context and is often used to convey a feeling of significance without any precise signification actually being intended. Environment is neither nature nor world—it is a scientifically constructed 'out there.' In speaking of an environmental crisis, therefore, we indicate both the problem and the attitude that underlies the problem.

We have an environmental crisis, because we treat the world as an environment. If we try to 'save' it, without at the same time challenging our assumptions about what it is, we will only drive these debilitating assumptions deeper into our culture.

The drought summer of 1988, when the hypothesis of global warming changed its scientific status from possible to probable, marked the beginning of an environmental panic that is likely to intensify over the next few years. By calling this growing alarm about the environment a panic, I don't mean to suggest that it has no basis but only to imply that a mood of fear and foreboding is unlikely to provide a stable basis for the kind of conversion that the crisis demands. In this kind of psychological climate, it is probable that the easier response to the crisis is likely to be the one taken, while the radical option will increasingly disappear from discussion. So we will get administrative controls, environmental services, a burgeoning new industry devoted to protecting the environment, and an ethos of resource efficiency that will allow economic assumptions to penetrate our lives more deeply than ever. Voluntary self-limitation, grounded in heart-felt and clear-sighted awareness of what our civilization has done, will come to seem an impractical revolutionary daydream that can't come to grips with the economy as it is.

This is sad, I think. The environmental crisis is the outward aspect of the corruption of human self-understanding, which results from a commodity-intensive, market-dominated way of life. It offers the opportunity for a deep questioning of this way of life. But if it is addressed superficially with damage-control measures, and ecology is used to paper over the cracks in the senile philosophy of economism, it will have been an opportunity missed. ◉

MICHAEL SRAGA

HEAVEN

The gate to heaven is bordered
with small round marquee lights,
some are missing,
some are broken,
some are burnt out.
The gate to heaven is made
from split and flattened aluminum cans
stapled together.

Above the gate is a marlin
arched to dive and mounted on
an always refreshing spray of sequins.
About all you can smell is
the burning narcotic of neglect.

Inside the gate there is a path
that takes you by a radio station
that broadcasts all your talents
and accomplishments
along with selections of your favorite music.
Instead of ads, illustrious historical figures
say they wish they could have been more like you.
Joan of Arc is speaking as you pass.

Beyond a barred door,
all notable religious figures are crammed into a closet,
formerly used for cleaning supplies.
They spend most of their time resting
or having visions of earth
but wake periodically to deliver their messages
to those gathered.

Every year they trade costumes.
Krishna gives Mary his abundant necklace of flowers
and blue pants,
and she gives him her long blue dress and veil.

You reach an Arabian tent,
pink and yellow billows of satin brilliance.
The linoleum path ends at the door.
Inside sits God at a card table
carefully examining two small salamanders.
He is heavy and not too tall,
with pale skin that doesn't fit well,
like butter just coming to bubble.
His shirt is yellow and looks Hawaiian
but instead of hula girls and leis
the pattern is made of double helixes
and cells frozen in the act of dividing.
God is in search of a low maintenance earth
so there is time to think of little else.

His forget-me-not eyes
are velvety and hard to read
with yellow centers and blue petals
that touch the eye sockets all round.
He asks you to sit down and offers a soda:
he must collect enough cans to build a wall to surround Heaven.
About you is the largest
salt and pepper shaker collection
you have ever seen.
Poodles, Statues of Liberty, men in sombreros
You know you are in the presence of God now.

In the distance you see God's house.
It sits on a platform raised 20 feet off the ground
which is covered with brambles
and broken beer bottles (no cans)
and half-eaten hard candies.
Two haloed lambs graze on long silver fishes
that grow straight up from the ground.

There is a satellite dish atop the shed.
Sometimes God wakes up late and forgets to unlock the spa door.
And sometimes he forgets
to tie his robe when he comes out on the porch
for a cigarette first thing in the morning.
All night he sits out on the patio in a twig chair
directing the universes with a wireless microphone
keeping light sleepers awake.

And on this path by God's house, there is nothing you cannot do.
There is no bondage of humanness.
No mountain from which you cannot spread your wings and fly.
No Italian car you cannot repair.
A dark spot appears in the sky,
a pellet in pastoral blue.
You walk toward it.
You reach a skinny man with no hair
holding a small ice cream scoop.
With one deft movement
he removes your soul from your body
like shucking an ear of corn
or twisting the head off a chicken.
Out of you is rescued
a clear shining blue light
like the bulbs on runways at night.
It travels across an aching blackness
and settles down in its place,
in a circle where it sits unblinking
brilliant, shining, free.

You rest in a place where
blue and purple and yellow pour from the sky.
Music written by gazelles
is played on orchids.
Peacock feathers soothe and bless with the thought of a breeze
Souls flourish in it like cattle.
Under it all is the low grind of a mixer churning
a batch of lemon snaps,
and singing om.

You know nothing
Not even enough to recognize that.
And God sits in his robe
in his twig chair, tired,
drinking scotch with a little ice
considering the possibilities.

MICHAEL SRAGA

HELL

There is a broad, high ceilinged
and welcoming entry hall.
In the entry area and the halls,
there are pictures on the walls.
What was best still
turned to life.
Stiff unto quivering
Vermeer Dutch ladies holding pitchers.
They turn to look at you as you pass
then hiss in Dutch to clean your room.
Soldiers charge down valleys
and kill each other again
and again so you are
waved ill by the blood
and the sound of the agonizing
celery crunch of bayonets.
A woman with one eye on her forehead
cries because she is deformed

and in pain
and if no one bought the artist's pictures
he wouldn't have kept doing this
to others.

The air is dessicated and slightly off scent.
The light, surgically bright.
Halfway down the hall,
an agent meets you.
She has tightly set blond hair
and wears a blue suit and bowed blouse.
She rolls a marble about in her mouth,
clicking it against her teeth.
She examines your ticket book
and pulls out a coupon.
At the door to the first room you are to visit
she taps dangerously with two long, curved blue fingernails.
You are bid to come in.
The office is not so small.
Behind the desk
there is a picture of a Keene woman
eating pastry from cellophane,
mouth sounds and crumbs
polluting the room.
The desk is dangerously organized,
as if someone with too much time were in charge.

Behind the desk there is an old lady,
though no one's mother.
She is pink and luminous like pearls,
delicate as if they were on a bad string.
She offers you cookies that
move about the plate
like lizards on a hot day
and asks how you're feeling now.
As if she knew how you'd felt before.

She puts a shell of a teacup
on a slip of a saucer
and sets it on the desk.
With her other hand she reaches for a delicate
blue porcelain teapot.
She nods at you, smiling,
then stands and holds the pot
high in the air
like a Moroccan in billows of enviable fabric.

And from the spout
you see a stream of
all the evil you committed.
Each as brilliant, as clear as
the closely etched Swiss countryside.
Symmetrical fields
and fences and mountains and cottages.
As breathtaking as an unexpected slap.

She watches the tea come out
and judges it as a connoisseur
then looks at you again.
The cats you pinched as a child, the cheating, the violence,
the inaction, every miscellaneous cruelty and deceit.

She offers you the tea.
It is more than polite to accept.
But you feel as if there were a fish
swimming through your body
blocking and flopping
everywhere at once.

She watches as you sip.
It is fetid, rank.
Fluid rats' heads and
all the way through you to tadpoles alive
under your fingernails, yet there is a ripple of inviting violet.
She watches you with abalone shell eyes
and files her nails

as you finish every silver drop
in the shimmering pot.

The agent meets you again and
delivers you to a dimly lit room,
big enough to build a house in.
You can see the walls
are padded with giant grey quilts.
You must walk on a net
drawn across the room
so there is
as much space below your feet
as above.
And you sit crouched on the net
until you realize
this is where you pay.
Balanced on the bouncing, rippling net you cry
tears of concentrated steaming acid,
scarring your face and body.

Soon your cries are cataclysmic.
You pull your knees to your chest
your body is raw and stinging.
It feels as if all your skin is being
stripped off in match-sized pieces.

You are a void, a vehicle
for the vibrations of pain.
The dialectic of being hacks at you
like a machete,
leaving immense ragged edges,
but there is gravity of
other worldly intensity.
There are stars within you
and stars without
and still the blood insists
on coursing through you.

The mesh of the netting
seems to be stretching
further apart.
You catch your finger
on a sharp part of a knot.
Soon, blood trickles spontaneously
from every pore outside,
every cell inside.
There's nothing to do,
blood spatters and winds
and twists everywhere.
It is pink foam.
Like a large dawn creek
in the mountains, too fast,
too turbulent to fish.

Nothing would keep you in
if you could get out.
You are held together only
by one singing, screaming
razor-edge ribbon of energy
that is Hell itself.

She comes to get you,
cool and somewhat disappointed,
but smiling.
She nearly touches your arm
as she leads you around
a long curved hallway lined with closed doors,
your ticket book in her hand.
She leaves you in a room
that is bare of clocks
or pictures
or windows.
She gets you water
and hands you aspirin in a paper packet.
Then she tears out the one coupon left.
That sends you back to live the life you just lived.

GALLERY

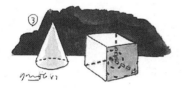

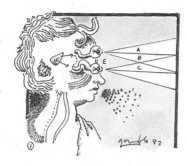

ERIC GAMBLE

ERIC GAMBLE

MIND JAZZ

*The noted cultural historian in conversation
with David Cayley, Tim Wilson,
Andrea Milinkovich, and Hilary Thompson.*

IN 1973, William Irwin Thompson left York University in Toronto to found the Lindisfarne Association. Disillusioned with the marginal role of the humanities in the modern multiversity, he wanted to create a 'contemplative community of scholars.' Thompson was interested in the planetization of humanity, a contemporary cultural epoch that he saw on the scale of great cultural transformations of the past, like the invention of agriculture or the rise of cities.

His new association took its name from the monastery off the coast of Northumbria that helped to spread Celtic Christianity through the dark centruies of the Viking Terror. Lindisfarne was sacked by the Norsemen in the year 793 but eventually the monks' vision flowered as a new civilization.

Thompson at first saw the new Lindisfarne on the same lines. Its task was to envision the arts and sciences of a new age and to recast the ideals of the dying age as a curriculum for the one being born. He wanted to bring together the isolated stars of a new age in order to show that they actually comprised a new constellation.

Lindisfarne at first was very diverse. Its guiding image of past-as-future attracted both Platonizing anti-modern elements and a group of forward-looking visionaries interested in new technologies and new philosophies of knowledge. But, by the mid-'80s, Thompson's own position had become clearer. Influenced by the work of cognitive biologists such as Gregory Bateson and the Chilean Francisco Varela, he became more and more willing to see ecology, and not a revived humanism, as the organizing metaphor of a new age. He concluded that his first understanding of Lindisfarne had been too defensive—still culture with a wall around it—and he began to see planetization almost entirely as an inevitable immaterial process to which he must simply trust himself.

One of the great influences on Thompson has been the work of scientists James Lovelock and Lynn Margulis, the originators of the Gaia Hypothesis. The theory arose from Lovelock's speculations about how the Earth's atmosphere can remain so far from the equilibrium, a state that it ought naturally to seek. He and Margulis eventually concluded that the entire biosphere is maintained by the biota for their collective benefit, that is, the biosphere as a whole acts as a single self-regulating entity. Corals building their undersea cities, and trees growing, are doing the work of Gaia by removing carbon dioxide from the atmosphere and thus allowing the Earth to maintain a constant temperature even as the sun gets hotter, as it has done during the course of evolution.

The Gaia Hypothesis got its name from a conversation between Lovelock and his neighbour, the novelist William Golding. Lovelock recounted the theory, and Golding proposed the name of the Greek earth goddess Gaia, wife of Uranus and mother of the gods. As a scientific hypothesis Gaia has remained controversial, but the name gave it a powerful cultural resonance; beginning from Paul Winter's composition, *Missa Gaia* (Earth Mass), in the early '80s, the theory has become widely known.

William Irwin Thompson is a storyteller, published as a poet and novelist as well as an historian; for him, Gaia is primarily a story, a myth by which the new planetary culture can be intuitively grasped. In 1987, he brought out a book called *Gaia: A Way of Knowing*, the proceedings of a Lindisfarne conference on the new biology, held the year before. Thompson's essays in the book use Gaia as a metaphor, relating the Earth as ecological process to a new theory of knowledge in which the dancer and the dance become indistinguishable, privileged perspectives disappear, and participation becomes everything.

In our conversation with Thompson, we began with the idea of Gaia as a way of knowing the world . . .

JWC Would you begin by talking about how and why you adopted the concept of Gaia? Perhaps beginning from Lovelock's work.

THOMPSON Some years ago, about 1976, when I was directing Lindisfarne, I gave four lectures on the future, which became my book *Darkness and Scattered Light*, and I remember making some sort of prediction about a new form of Darwinian synthesis that would provide us with a scientific narrative to connect the little and the large.

I had heard of the Gaia Hypothesis and read just the brief papers that had appeared. I had not met Jim Lovelock or Lynn Margulis. At the time I had an itch beyond the reach of scratch that there was something needed in the culture and I was trying to think my way toward it, which is the intuitive way I generally work. I kept working in that field because the project of Lindisfarne has always been to try to connect ecology, spirituality, and intellectuality in ways that were not possible at the MIT, or at York for that matter, as York was a suburban drive-in university.

So, when I read Jim Lovelock's book *Gaia* in '79 and then read *Symbiosis and Cell Evolution* by Lynn Margulis in '81, I really was taken with them. This was thinking on a planetary scale that was precisely the kind of way to reconceptualize the ecology and politics for the 21st century.

So I invited Jim Lovelock and Lynn Margulis to come to Lindisfarne, and then Humberto Maturana and Francisco Varela from Santiago, Heinz and Elaine Pagels from New York, and Henri Atlan from the French school of self-organizing systems biology. These people hadn't met before.

My mind just flashed with visions—this was what I was looking for. If one adopted the shift in perception that was built into the Gaia Hypothesis, then very practical problems could be seen in new ways. For instance, if there was to be a shift in our politics from ideology to ecology, then we couldn't empower a single elite: we had to have disparate people brought together. And if we were going to go beyond the idea of the nation state as occupying a piece of turf, we had to look upon identities coming from living processes and to see people as endosymbionts in a cell, sharing a process, not a turf.

If you look in a classical way, then identity comes from an object. It may be a subatomic particle or a discrete gene that can be manipulated to give you an object containing value. Value is stored in objects, be they banks or museums. Therefore you have to defend value against intrusions to the object, whether the object is the museum or the bank or a territorial nation state.

If you shift your thinking and see that identity is coming from a process—you are not fixing your identity from a piece of turf—then you become like an endosymbiont. *Endosymbiont* is another word for a good neighbour within a cell. The metaphor for this is the mitochondria, the little critters that crawled into our cells ages ago that have their own DNA (their own identity) and produce oxygen for our cells.

If the Palestinians and the Israelis, or the Northern and Southern Irish, or the Sikhs and Singhalese and Sri Lankans started thinking in that way, then our politics would be less homicidal. This is the paradigm shift that has to happen. Ecology has begun to be the real political science of the future for me.

Part of Lynn's work has been to question the patriarchial narratives of biology: that value is in a discrete gene, that genes are passed on by competing males, and females are merely receptacles for taking in the male genes—a kind of sociobiological narrative. She said, 'No, the female's sharing in symbiosis and these processes is as much a part of the architecture of the evolution of the cell as any.'

Ten or twelve years ago this was a very radical hypothesis. Now it is respected, and Margulis is considered one of the great living American biologists. It hasn't yet filtered into the political thinking, because we are still caught up in this old idea that the truth can be expressed by a single being, a great mind, who will articulate it with an elite who will share the ideology. The elite will enforce the ideology to the mass, and that will give you a revolution for the good. That, I think, is a really violent form of thought that does violence to truth and to people and nations. It leads to things such as Iran or the Soviet Union, which is now coming apart from ideological thinking.

The main idea in Lovelock is that worlds embrace repulsions: processes that seem to be violently opposed can be constitutive of other architectures of order. So one animal's excrement becomes the food for another bacteria. The planet is a delicately balanced thing between the fixed and the fluid. For example, the continental plates are fixed over time and the gaseous atmosphere is fluid. So a healthy living system, such as ours with our fixed skeleton and our fluid rivers of blood, has to embrace these opposites.

JWC So, you ventured into this new science looking for political and philosophical resonance?

THOMPSON I first entered as an artist. I'm fascinated by horizon and edges, and hence the title *At the Edge of History*. So my first engagement has always been a literary one. If nature is more complicated than we once thought, then I can't be an artist by going out and painting and writing a poem to nature. So my way of writing poetry has been to change the role of the artist in the cybernetic culture. Rather than reading my poetry, I would give talks that would be presentations of ideas. That was radically different than being Allen Ginsberg or Robert Bly and giving a reading of one's poems.

I had to change the definition of what it means to be a bard in an electronic culture. In a traditional culture, a bard is the recitor of the identity of the past. I have tried to change it to make the bard the invoker of the identity of the future.

I tried to take the impulse of the bardic imagination and say, 'If identity isn't based on turf, and if identity is a process and it can be invocatory of cultures that are emerging, how can I be sensitive to the horizons of what is going on?'

This began to change the nature of poetry for me to a kind of mind jazz, playing with other jazz musicians such as Margulis, Varela, and Lovelock. Taking their works and showing them connections that they didn't see and then inspiring them (they've all become friends, so I'm a great date-a-mate service). So it's more of an artistic, aesthetic function. Shelley said the poets are the unacknowledged legislators of humanity.

JWC What does the Gaia Hypothesis say to our more traditional ideas of nature? That is, the objective existence of nature.

THOMPSON First of all, it says that nature is an arbitrary threshold. You cut a square in the universe and you stand on the bottom of that square and you call what's on the other side of the window 'nature.' But where are you going to cut that square? At the molecular level, and see the entrancing dance of molecules and

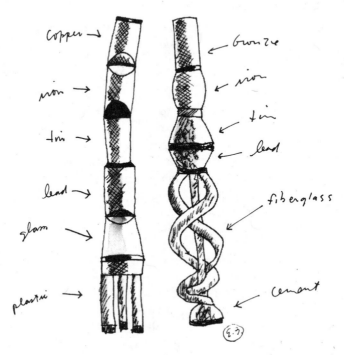

flashing electric skins and light that at another level might be pollution? This beautiful vision you are having of the dance of molecules in nature might be a New Jersey toxic dump! But inside it, at the molecular level, it could be wonderfully natural! Or, you could be at the level of a supernova, exploding and creating havoc, and that can be nature too.

When we say 'nature,' we are really influenced by the Sierra Club calendars, the photos of Ansel Adams who is influenced by Constable and Gainsborough—it is a kind of 18th-century, gentlemanly vision of the great estate in the park. That is a cultural idea, it has nothing to do with nature.

In the 19th century, nature was objective. The observer was subjective. By decreasing subjective contamination, you could achieve a reading of nature that was pure and true. And the most pure was where the human was least present! (We now have the same idea—only we call it Deep Ecology—that nature in its most pure state is not contaminated by trailer parks, by weekend hikers, by selling pharmaceuticals from the Amazon.) Nature at its purest is an uncontaminated state.

But there is no such thing as that nature; that's fiction! Nature is the horizon of culture. Every time you change cultures, you change the horizons. Nature in a shamanic culture might have angels and elementals and spirits. In a Hopi culture, a holy spirit would ensoul the sacred mountain. Then the shaman, going into meditation, would commune with the mountain and have a vision. Imagine the cyberpunk world of *Neuromancer* by William Gibson. Nature in a cyberpunk landscape might have machines that were ensouled by *entelechies* [vital forces directing growth and life] and the Druid wizard who was jacking into cyberspace would begin to commune with the spirit that had ensouled that mechanism. Here we are getting into the sci-fi world of the 'unnatural.'

Now for us in our 19th-century romantic world, we think nature is trees and mountains; but that *other* technology—*that* is abhorrent, evil, unnatural. But I think if one really wants to understand what is going on in the shifting horizons of our culture, one has to understand nature as going in two directions simultaneously. One is the return to nature with the Greens, and the other is the destruction of 'nature' in the cyberpunk landscape with things such as *Bladerunner* or *Neuromancer*. Unless you look at both of those edges of our culture and ask yourself 'What is nature?' I don't think you'll really see the transformation that is going on right under your nose.

Let me give you Lynn Margulis' example of what nature is. She says all the environmentalists come to Boston and they say Boston Harbour is dead; it's polluted. She says, 'No, I see all my friends out there'—meaning all the bacteria she studies—'and they are chewing the tires and frolicking in the oil slick.'

So nature is a fiction. The only precise way you can define it is: there is no such thing as nature; nature is the horizon of culture. Whatever state you are in, and whatever human activity, you will always have a horizon.

JWC Are you saying that the end of nature as an idea is simply the end of the Constable vision of nature?

THOMPSON Yes, the anthropocentric view. I don't feel threatened by technology because I know, being a city kid, most of my mystical experiences in my life have come from things like watching *Fantasia* when I was five, listening to Tchaikovsky on the radio when I was seven, listening to Beethoven string quartets on LP when I was recovering from surgery in high school. So there have been all these mystical experiences that have been mediated by technology.

I don't find technology a threat. That's why I really like David Spangler, who is a Lindisfarne fellow, because he's a totally whacked out, deep-space mystic, but he's got computers all over his house. He's a total hacker!

JWC Isn't the end of nature the end of natural selection? The important thing is not just the end of nature as artists and the Romantics conceived it, but also as certain scientists have conceived it and how we've conceived of evolution.

THOMPSON Nature in the new way of thinking would be seen like a Prigogine fluid dynamic.

What you get is that animals, through their metabolic processes that are shared in a common phase space, extrude an evolutionary landscape. Their excretions, inhalations, etc., are creating a kind of dialogue through time. They climb on top of one another's niches, and one will create a form of pollution that is a disaster and the other one will scurry around very quickly and begin to adapt over time. So the dance of life is seen more as what Varela calls natural drift, rather than adaptation.

The old notion 'you have to adapt or you're going to die' has its identity in a gene that you can manipulate and in an organism that must adapt to its niche—which is clamped into its niche. But in Prigogine biology, the organisms are actually dancing, and they are extruding their environment.

It is like a river that is sculpting its banks at the same time that the banks are shaping the river. The landscape emerges!

You have to change your language, so Varela uses lovely poetic language such as 'brought forth.' Worlds are brought forth. Or you use concepts of emergence. So the particular evolutionary landscape that is brought forth is radically different at each particular time. And nature is changing all through this.

In this period of time, you can say we are moving from natural selection to cultural intrusion. There are various ways of changing the atmosphere with the greenhouse effect, or the ozone hole. We have created an invisible environment of electronic noise. We are in a totally invisible environment of electronic pollution that is having a direct effect on our nervous systems and some people are being selected out, if you add the effects up for 100 or 200 years. Those who were good at living with trees are on their way out, and those who are good at living with video display terminals and silicon tubes will be selected for. So cultures are actually selecting for a new post-natural environment in which the dance may be beyond imagination of what nature may be in the 21st century.

JWC How then can ecology provide the moral dimension in political science that you said it would?

THOMPSON Ecology is studying processes within our horizon. How does a cell work? How does a swamp work? How does a marsh work? How do biological processes enter into a dialogue? How do they interact with human beings?

We have studied ecology and said, 'Okay, we can see that it is an industrial, cultural mentality to come in and level Kansas and put in wheat.' But the prairie now operates in a different way and has a more complex dialogue. You don't want to romanticize and say, 'It was purer when the Indians were there,' because they came in and had prairie fires. They burned out a lot of the higher vegetation and, as much as we can tell, created stampedes using fire to drive all the animals over a cliff and have a huge slaughter. It is called the extinction of the Pleistocene megafauna. So, there were intrusions on nature in the period of 9000-8000 BC. The Indians were the only inhabitants of this continent, and they were doing stuff that was changing nature. They were sculpting the prairies. Everywhere we look in nature we see processes like that going on.

Part of bringing Varela together with Margulis was seeing that if your body is perceived as a container of value, then the typical way of regarding the immune system is that it is your army fighting the aliens on the beach. But there have been very interesting experiments showing that if a mouse gets meningitis, it dies, but if you infect a pregnant mouse with meningitis, the fetus does not react to the meningitis as an alien. In other words, its immune system is not triggered to read the presence of that alien as a threat. Not reading it as a threat, it doesn't treat it as a pathogen, an invading object. It treats it as a relationship, it does not get the disease and does not die!

So if you can tolerate aliens, whether they are Mexicans or viruses, you end up with a totally different endosymbiotic relationship. You end up with a situation that is much healthier. Our thinking in our culture for the last couple of centuries since the Industrial Revolution has had some ideas in it that are pernicious. And we are now beginning to see that they are bankrupt, they are failing in every level from agri-business to political science.

JWC I have the impression that Lynn Margulis was very resistant from the beginning, and I would suspect still is, to the humanization of Gaia, the Earth, as a sentient, conscious, human-like being.

THOMPSON In the hermeneutics of popular movements, there have always been mistakes. First of all, to call Gaia an organism makes us unable to perceive higher-order, biotic processes. So she is a little resistant to that. It might be more interesting to say: What is this meta-domain in which organisms constitute a higher biological activity?

Then so many people associated Gaia with the Goddess of neolithic culture and with certain forms of mysticism, which was for her just a kind of muddy thinking. But primarily Lynn is not anthropocentric. She really wants to extend her vision of life to include the bacteria as constituents of life as we know it. We always want to take them for granted.

I remember the first time I was in India. I was shocked that people in Indian culture didn't see the servants or the women. They were standing at the door, watching us eat and they weren't allowed to sit at the table with us. I kept seeing servants and women and wanted to establish relations with them but that was forbidden in terms of their culture. It is the same thing with bacteria. So Lynn says, 'No, this will not do.'

The implications of that in terms of architecture are that if you go to a bad architecture school they say, 'Here is the land; you put a building on it. It is to serve a corporation and your ego and to make a profit.' If you begin to think in terms of Margulis' work, then you say: 'A building should not be built on the ground but out of the processes that it excretes. What is its shadow? What is its pollution? What is the full description of its nature?' Then you create a bacterial membrane that is the definition between your social purpose and the shadow and excretion of the building.

That kind of architecture would be so radical and so healthy that the air of our cities would change. The water, which is so toxic, would change; and you would have a whole generation of biological membrane architecture that would look radically different from the banks and insurance buildings that dot the landscape from Toronto to Sydney. So it is extremely revolutionary thinking. It changes everything.

JWC Do you see any danger in losing rootedness, embodiment, or a sense of place by adopting this ecology of consciousness?

THOMPSON   I guess that's why I've always been involved in contemplative practices.

I had this argument with Wendell Berry once at Lindisfarne in Colorado. Wendell is a close friend and a Lindisfarne fellow. We've all been thinking out loud in these jam sessions for the last twelve years. Wendell was going on about his rootedness and the spirit of place. His family has been in Henry County, Kentucky, for nine generations. I am more an electron than a nucleus; I don't have a location. So I am almost Wendell's exact opposite. I have a tendency to feel that I am deracinated, unnatural, unrooted, have no sense of identity, that I am your typical uprooted, academic, nomadic intellectual.

I remember feeling frustrated. I said, 'Damn it, Wendell, you keep talking about "place," but I see the monarch butterflies heading for Mexico and I see the hummingbirds leaving me for the winter, and over the horizon I can imagine the whales heading south. It wasn't the rich that invented this lifestyle—it was "animals in nature." So what is all this stuff?'

As a matter of fact, the 19th-century farm is perhaps one more disastrous imposition on nature. If we go back to 9000 BC, we have hunting, gathering, and fishing, and we don't have value fixed so much in location. It was the increasing surplus of grains that allowed us to start holding food in containers and then surrounding our buildings with walls. Then men could take their

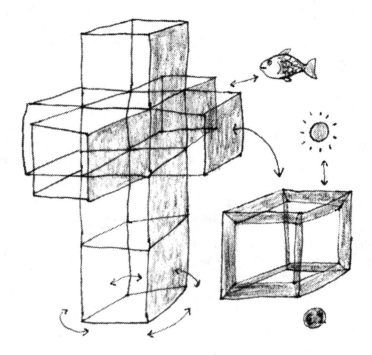

hunting bows and arrows and use them for raids. And raids grew into warfare. Thus, agriculture, the fixing of value in turf, is inseparable from militarism.

If you think more contemplatively, you say, 'I don't draw my identity from fixed turf or from my meat body. I find my identity much more involved in complex topological processes that move in more than three dimensions.' There is no way to map that, except in higher math or mysticism. Those opposites are crossing in our culture—mathematicians such as Ralph Abraham of the Chaos Dynamic crowd are very mystical guys. This enables me to live in a way that might be disorienting for someone who is in a 19th-century family farm.

JWC You've mentioned Yoga and you've had some involvement with Buddhism. Is there a natural affinity between what you've been talking about so far and the Eastern religions? As opposed to the Judeo-Christian traditions.

THOMPSON The project of Romanticism (God knows I spent most of my life in that project since I grew up on Yeats and Dylan Thomas) has been to try to humanize industrial technology with art and to make a religion out of art. But eventually art fails, it just isn't powerful enough to do that.

I think the importation of the contemplative traditions of the East—Zen and Tibetan Buddhism and Yoga—was to provide the real romanticism for electronic technology. So Zen and Buddhism and Yoga are to electronic technology what Wordsworth was to the railroads—the necessary Yeatsian complement to create a real, full culture. I don't think you can humanize electronic technology with anything less. Being a good Presbyterian or Anglican is just not powerful enough to handle the forces of the electronic world—computers, space travel, the disintegration of the natural as we have been defining it.

JWC So what about the hardy band of Jews and Christians who are now back into their tradition trying to find a relation to ecology there?

THOMPSON On one hand you have nativists and fundamentalist movements and on the other, you have the rediscovery of the mystical. People such as Father William McNamara and Sister Tessa Bialeci—Roman Catholic contemplatives and friends of mine—would say: If you are really sensitive to contemplative practice, then you can read the Gospel of John and see all kinds of things in it that you would not see if you were going to a conventional Sunday school. There is a great deal of repressed mystical tradition in the West that got swept under the carpet. So part of any cultural movement is always to have a reinvention of the past. Every revolution is preceded by a revisioning of history.

I think that the reason the dialogue between Buddhism and Christianity has been so powerful is that it is very easy for the Abrahamic and Vedic religions to get fixed. They are a little more crystalline and can lead to fundamentalisms of ideological hysteria all too easily. But the quality of planetization, to use Chardin's phrase, would include a Buddhist sense of space—because their cosmology is just so sci-fi and vast—and a Christian sense of time.

If you have a Buddhist sense of cosmology then there is no creation—it's always been going on, and there is no end of history.

There are innumerable universes trembling at the tip of Buddha's hair. But basically they don't place a great deal of emphasis on the temporality of history. If you are a Christian, you have this great narrative: the creation, the fall, the redemption, the *Parousia* [advent] waiting for us at the end of time. There is this whole drama that we have to do something *now* in order to achieve the purpose of our incarnation. So the whole notion of Kairos and epiphany, of the intense value that we place on being incarnate in historical time, and that history carries the momentum of our incarnation— this is a very Western value. As an Irishman caught up in the myths of history, I sort of share that sensibility, but I think that the two can come together. I think those two are coming together in the crucible of North America, and the dialogue between Buddhism and science is a particularly exciting one.

JWC You referred several times to your colleague Francisco Varela. Who is he and what is his new biology?

THOMPSON Varela is a cognitive scientist; he's a neurophysiologist. He's involved in a branch of cognitive science that is called 'connectionism,' which is trying to create slower computers with fuzzy logic that think analogically like the human brain, as opposed to fast computers that think digitally with gates of off-on, 1-0. The only way they can achieve the complexity is through parallel distributive processing, as the ideas in the brain are not simply located in one cell. They are located in a distributive lattice that organizes the brain into a domain or a state. So Varela is studying this stuff in his institute for neurosciences in Paris.

We've been working together on a program for biology, cognition, and ethics over the last three years and have written four books together. He is a colleague who has greatly influenced my thinking. He enabled me to make the connection between cognitive science and the Gaia Hypothesis. What I'm trying to do is connect ecology and biology and cognitive science and political science.

JWC Can you make a start at how you see that connection?

THOMPSON If Gaia is a system of learning that maintains itself over time, then parallel distributive processing, connectionist lattices and emergent states that have the capacity to learn are precisely what we're talking about when we're dealing with Gaia.

Varela has also studied the immune system, and from another avenue you could almost define Gaia as the immune system of the planet that maintains its self-ness, its self-identity, over time. So you can look at Gaia at the atmospheric level with Lovelock's work in atmospheric chemistry, as the macrocosm. Then you can look at the microcosm of the bacteria with Lynn Margulis, where she will argue that bacteria are not distinct species but are one superorganism, which gives you a planetary bioplasm. When you study the immune system in the individual, you see a particular entity that isn't a discrete object but is like an enclouded self that is maintaining, through the blood and the marrow, a definition of selfhood over time where the self really begins to be the phase space of the body. (In the same way if you studied the Foucault pendulum, its phase space is larger than the ball.) And so you see in all three how a metadynamic can emerge from a highly connected system, so that it begins to be self-naming, autonomous, and maintains that autonomy and identity over time.

It begins to be really fascinating. What you can do is say: Here are four domains in which I wish to study that—the nervous system with the brain, the immune system, the bacterial bioplasm of the planet, and the atmosphere. In order to understand those, because they are processes and not objects, you need a new geometry in order to perceive them. My old geometry asks me to look for an object; I have to be able to nail it down to a discrete hunk of matter. But this is saying, 'No, a phase space is not an object; you need not think in terms of Euclidian geometry but in terms of Chaos Dynamics. You need a whole new geometry of phase portraits to perceive what's happening.'

If you take the mesocosm of the mind, it's the meeting place for the macrocosm of the atmosphere in Lovelock and the microcosm of the bacterial bioplasm with Margulis. Then if you look at their behaviours, you say, well, they're all funny. They have something of the same shape—they're homeomorphic. What is the shape of the atmosphere with Lovelock? What is the shape of the bioplasm with Margulis? What is the shape of the immune system with Varela? Then you realize they are not objects. Their shape has a totally different quality. You need a new mathematical imagination in order to perceive it. Well, lo and behold, there just happens to be out there on the horizon a new math imagination coming in from the Chaos Dynamics crowd. And so we invited Ralph Abraham, the elder statesman of the Chaos Dynamics crowd, to Lindisfarne. All of us come together to share imaginations so we can begin to perceive what are the shapes that are going on out there in the horizon.

So when you say nature, I say, 'What is the shape of nature in your imagination?' I rather imagine it has been influenced by Eliot Porter, Ansel Adams, Gainsborough, and Constable.

JWC What I see on the horizon, in the wake of the perception of an ecological, environmental crisis, is an age of technocracy, not an age of poets-as-legislators, as you mentioned earlier. If you look at the redefinition of the World Bank in the last few years, now it wants to offer environmental services. If you think of the papers emanating from the United Nations and the World Watch Institute, the word of the day is planetary management. The ideal is technocratic—the opposite of what you have been talking about!

THOMPSON No it's not the opposite! First, notice they are adopting our language, which means their old language is no longer effective. When Wes Jackson was giving a lecture at a college and they exploded into applause, Walter Mondale quickly looked around and said, There's a movement here! He thought he could help lead the movement. Now that we realize we no longer have the Russians as an enemy, we have to find something else to keep big science going. It is the environment. The chaps at MIT are very straightforward. Their approach is: Give us the big bucks and we'll shoot down the ozone hole for you. We'll put up Star Wars, zap the ozone hole with molecules, and fight the environment, as LBJ fought poverty. Naturally there is no change of thinking there; they don't realize that if you think like Gregory Bateson or Wes Jackson or John Todd, you don't come up with that shoot-'em-down mentality. The American, manipulative, kick-the-tires kind of practical 'I'm from Missouri—show me' science is just bullshit!

But I take heart from Margulis' work, because she has pointed out in *Symbiosis and Cell Evolution* that when the cell evolved, some of its constituents came from the engorgement of entities trying to digest and eat one another. They were predatory relationships, where a hunk of gunk surrounded something with the idea of eating it! But, it couldn't break down its membrane and it ended up staying inside the cell, like the mitochondria or the chloroplast, and became part of the architecture of a much more complicated entity.

So, MIT and the big corporations and the nation states are all trying to co-opt the environmental movement, and the first step is to co-opt the language, but not to have a change of mind—to resist the metanoia. But that's human nature. You have to look in terms of thousands of years. They will try to break down our membrane and digest us and we'll either get broken down and digested or we won't. We'll end up with an endosymbiont, complex ecology that will be quite different from the World Bank mentality and that is very different from the '60s and '70s.

The old people say we need a world state and we need to have centralized control. But if you've got these new biological imaginations, you understand that more complex learning systems don't organize themselves with centre-periphery geometries; they work through distributive lattices and processes. So the last thing on Earth we want is a single state in charge of the biosphere. But the old people who had this other mentality will just have this knee-jerk reaction. I think there is another generation coming up that has a more subtle imagination. I have faith!

But sure, it is going to be a hockey face-off in the '90s. I'm not saying that just the people holding the daisies will take over the Earth—'The meek will inherit the Earth.' I'm enough of an Irishman with a tragic sense of history not to fall sucker to that one.

JWC It seems to me that at one time you yourself may have held some contradictions together.

THOMPSON I'm sure I still hold contradictions because I think you couldn't have a brain or a complex personality unless you embraced opposites. I think the creative process is inherently one of the dance of opposites. It's a complex kind of alchemy. Any other simplifying ideology always falsifies one side of our nature.

JWC Aside from cyberpunk, if you look for evil as the shadow of the emergent shape of the next ecology, where would you find it?

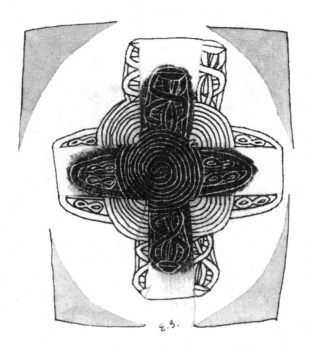

THOMPSON I can see the New Age getting really crypto-fascist. I was really appalled when I discovered some of the really reactionary things going on in Deep Ecology, that it was based on a hatred of the human and a lack of compassion and a racism I was unhappy with. And some of my friends were very much into trying to achieve the sacred as the fixed, that the sacred was eternal and the fallen was the moving, and the only way you could achieve the sacred was with a class that was attuned to the eternal and unchanging—namely a caste system.

I remember an argument in London with Keith Critchlow, who is not a reactionary but a kind of Summerhill-educated, English Labour Party socialist and yet is committed to the Platonic idea. He pointed to his watch and said, 'The centre is fixed,' and that all the world of temporality and change and appearance just goes round and round. And there was the idea that nothing is ever new; values are fixed.

I had a deep experience in meditation one day where all that just died to me—like a real death experience. I could feel a metanoia where my mentality changed and I moved out of that. Then intellectually I began to understand and appreciate that there was a new mathematics on the horizon that was part and parcel of the *true* New Age. Not this medieval Platonism.

When I set up Lindisfarne, with a Dark Age metaphor, to preserve knowledge in an age of change or loss, it was an attempt to bring together artists and scientists, poets and painters, and to hold on to some levels of culture in a period when we were just getting the Shirley MacLaine of everything. Its model was defensive of identity—it was us versus them. I think that was unimaginative and inappropriate on my part. It was too narrow and didn't understand the larger process.

If I invested my identity in that, I'd be a bitter intellectual hating the modern world. I see degradation as a digestion process—and even Shirley MacLaine has her way of signalling that the New Age movement is over. Now that it is getting broadcast everywhere, it is time to let it go and move on to other things. Now I can feel less threatened and less paranoid. But so many intellectuals I know look with scathing contempt on the fallen world and just wait for some apocalypse to cleanse it. ◉

THE LANGUAGE OF
SKIN CREAMS

A WOMAN ON HER WAY to buy manila envelopes finds herself threading through the ground floor of a large department store. Islands of cosmetics, with their dense, tiny pots of promise and ziggurats of skin-care products, stand in her way. As she tacks this way and that, certain phrases assail her: 'Anti-aging cell repair,' 'Moisture Recharging Complex,' 'Renewal Night Treatment.' Is this the Mayo Clinic or the make-up department, she wonders, slowing but not stopping. She passes another display that promises 'Total Time Fighting Care.' Hmmm. Triumph over time, in a jar . . . yes! She veers over to the time cream, palms the heavy sea-green tester, and begins to lubricate herself.

Behind the counter is a lustrous clerk in a white lab coat with a cardboard computer, ready to evaluate the thirst and carnage of her skin. The woman, normally immune to the lure of rabbit-decimating lipsticks and redundant eyeshadows, nevertheless finds herself listening to the clerk, fascinated by her curved and combed eyebrows, as she describes the 'biomimetic activity' of the cream's 'anti-aging emollients.' These are not simple creams, but advanced, inscrutable, scientific systems and oh, for a system, any system, in these unravelling times. Plus, the woman is forty, over forty, and has taken to spotting the strange, pointy, post-facelift jawlines on late-night talk shows.

All around her the beauty stakes are being upped every day. She smooths some time-fighter on the heartless clock of her face, looks in the mirror, and imagines her face stopping. A subtle feeling, like burrowing termites, fizzes under the skin around her eyes. Obviously this is Science at work. So she peels off forty-five—or sixty-five—dollars, and drifts away, excited, flushed,

 ashamed, having bribed Time itself and become her own Dr. Frankenstein. In just a few weeks, the brochure says, her skin will be 'fresher, younger, and more organized.' Organized skin! No more slovenly, haphazard aging! She feels so optimistic that when she hits the stationery department she buys a colourful desktop file system she will fill and never use.

Strange that this woman, who knows her nitrates from her nitrites and can spot 'Red Dye No. 3' on a food label from ten yards, should fall for an overpriced wrinkle cream described in pseudo-scientific mumbo jumbo. Perhaps it was the quaint lure of that phrase 'scientifically formulated'—as if such mysteries could still be bought. The fact is, she feels a little sorry for science; physics has uncrowned it, mixed it up with fiction, mysticism, and philosophy. Pure pockets of hardcore scientific religiosity are hard to find. The 'scientifically formulated' allure depends on the notion that this cream will act upon you in a way that is powerful, unknowable, and best left to experts. It exacts from us a 'faith in facts' based on sheer, exhilarating ignorance. The point of the skin-cream ad copy is to befuddle and impress; if it's 'scientific,' it must be true. The woman knows this to be false, but it's a slightly more flattering pitch than, say, 'Get a man before your face turns into the Alberta badlands.'

Let us take a closer look at this intelligent but susceptible envelope-shopper. She wears little or no make-up, and studiously buys non-violent banana oils at The Body Shop. However, she also suffers from a mild shopping disorder that flares up occasionally, like malaria. It strikes her when she least expects it. Perhaps she's a little depressed. Perhaps she feels that the job of being female entails far too much measuring up, beset as she is by images of youth and beauty on TV and in magazines. She remembers the first time The Pitch got under her skin (as it were). She was on her way through a store, again. She passed the Clinique counter— the word 'clinique' a clever coinage suggesting a boutique of science, a lab of beauty. She saw the women dressed like technicians, with plain, efficient, minimal-gender jars that featured words, not images. And the phrase that hooked her was 'Moisture Surge.'

A hit, a fix, a surge of humidity. For all its prim packaging, the phrase had an unavoidable eroticism. (Did the marketing people consider 'Wet Swoon?') So she swerved over to the counter, and picked up the heavy pink tester, with its mute silvery lid. This was obviously not some passive little cream you slap on in the morning but a powerful CEO of a hydrating honcho who won't take no for an answer from your skin. She read the 'literature' that came with the 'system.' The subtitle was 'The Intensifier.' Yes, intensify me, by all means, she thought. Make vivid my Hudson's Bay life. She read on. 'Moisture Surge is a lightweight gel with new-tech speed and skill.' New-tech presumably comes after hi-tech, from the root *technology*, meaning good, superior, perfect. And skill! An intelligent emollient, a cream with a resumé! 'Used in addition to the regular Clinique system of skin care' (more $$$) 'it sparks a quick surge of extra power.'

A quick surge of extra power. She peeled off forty-two dollars and took the jar home where it sat with a radioactive aura on a bathroom shelf. For days she avoided using it. What if . . . it oversurged? What if her face became too empowered with mois-ture and swelled up like a watermelon? Instead, she found herself sitting on the toilet every morning, rereading the literature and the label. And the remarkable thing was . . . her skin improved. Nightly scanning of magazine ads also visibly reduced the tiny lines around her eyes. She discovered that the words themselves had a deep penetrating action that actually enhanced her cell cohesiveness.

Time passed, despite the cream. She discovered the next 'scientific' hook, microspheres—visible blobs of 'active in-gredients' suspended in a clear gel. It was a childlike way to make the cream look more complicated and powerful, as if she were gazing into the molecular blueprint under a microscope. She found the word 'microspheres' increased the blood supply to her skin surface within hours. She then bought Niosôme's Système Anti-Âge, which had special microspheres with 'niosomes,' which, the literature assured

her, were 'anti-aging actives.' The sheer opacity of such a claim reassured her, the way elves and tooth fairies once did.

Then, one day when she wasn't so thrilled with her relationship, or her work, or her shoes, she went out and bought Esteé Lauder's 'Time Zone' . . . 'the rich, soufflé crème so influential it can reprogram the future of dry skin.' It was silly, she knew, but she longed to be reprogrammed. The ad copy suggested that if 'Time Zone' couldn't precisely stop time, it could still bargain effectively with the future. 'Time Zone'—an executive cream from a good family, with money and power, come to manage your skin and arm it for the future—the future, as Esteé so bluntly put it, of dry skin. She rubbed it in, the genie cream, and felt noticeably younger and wetter.

Science used to measure the material world. But the closer and longer it looked, the more the world dematerialized. Now we live in a 'new-tech' medieval kingdom of waves, impulses, fission, and transaction that has disembodied us, leaving us with the lightness of being, a modem, and . . . dry skin. Drat! she thinks. If it's the end of history, then what are those lines on my face? We need something to erase this troubling reminder of our corporeality. Something to rub in and rub us out. Why be half-disembodied? So she gathered up all the jars and vials, and put them out by the curb in the blue recycling box. But she kept all the labels and boxes. It was language, she discovered, not science, that fought off time, and kept on working all night long. ◉

URBAN WILDLIFE

HOUSE MOUSE (*Mus musculus*)

ABOUT EVERY TWO WEEKS or so I kick a mouse out of the house. For a long time I had been finding the little caraway seed-like turds in all the usual disgusting places—such as the hollows of spoons and the toothbrush glass. The sweet smell of mouse pee had become almost ambient. My husband's eyebrows had begun jerking together hard and often. So I sought out and found a Ketch-All, guaranteed to catch up to fifteen mice at one setting.

The Ketch-All is an aluminum box containing a sort of paddle-wheel flipper. When the mouse goes in the hole in the side—and mice can't help but go in the sides of things—it steps on a spring. The spring launches the paddle-wheel and the mouse is scooped up and deposited unharmed in a holding room. The manufacturers of the Ketch-All also offer an accessory 'drowning device.'

But I can't drown a mouse. For the life of me I can't work up the ferocious indignation I'm supposed to feel as a human who's had her dishrags gnawed on. I just can't. So, after they're caught, my mice simply get the old heave-ho. I slide up the sliding section of the Ketch-All (designed to be slid up for sliding out the miserable little bodies of drowned mice) and they skitter out the door, down the alley, under a mousey pile of leaf-and-litter. Shortly to return, of course—but maybe not without having first had their reproductive habits somewhat disordered.

Some house mice are gay, which came as a surprise to *me*. Each family group is dominated by the biggest, strongest male who, needless to say, gets all the females all the time. So the littler males start to notice each other and start to like what they see.

Daytime is a good time to see a homosexual mouse, if you're looking. For not only do the big, strong males get all the females,

they also get first nocturnal dibs on all the crumbs under the toaster, the pear in the fruit bowl, and the plastic that wrapped the sticky Danish. When mice sneak out under cover of darkness, the main men lead the way, nibbling and gnawing and dribbling their musty trail of urine. They mark out their territory as dogs do. They tend to eat more than is strictly fair.

Lowlier mice must resort to unnatural diurnal habits, creeping out in the morning or the quiet of the afternoon. Their forays, dangerously visible to begin with, are made more dangerous by the terrible lack of caution with which they are conducted. I've seen daytime mice approach within inches of my sleeping dog's muzzle. I've seen them sprint across the counter while I opened the fridge for the mustard. The Ketch-All always catches more mice by day than by night.

It's come nowhere close, however, to catching numbers such as the estimated 132,000 per hectare that chewed crops in the Central Valley of California in the '20s. Mice breed at an exhausting rate, and females may have up to fourteen litters of anywhere between three and sixteen young in one year. Since they arrived from Europe on the ships of the conquistadors, their skill at breeding, eating ethnic, and squeezing themselves almost flat has made them the most common rodents in Canada. There are more

Canadian mice than there are of all other rodents put together.

They can oversucceed, however. And when they do, and they become confined and crowded, two things happen: first, the adolescent females become infertile, and second, mice of both sexes begin to bite.

There's an article in an 1889 issue of *The American Naturalist* that talks about a special feature of mice appreciated by the Victorians but seldom mentioned since. The article is 'Musical Mouse' and in it, the author, W.O. Hickey, describes a mouse in the back of a closet singing over a shoe filled with popcorn. The mouse would sit among his popcorn and 'sing his beautiful solo for ten minutes at a time.' The song went like this: *to-wit-to-wee-to-woo-woo-wee-woo*. A beautiful song. I wish I could have heard it.

I looked up the derivation of the word 'mouse' and here it is: Old English *mus*, from the Sanskrit *musha* meaning 'thief.' *Not*, as our typically deceptive English spelling would suggest, and my own naive romantic notions would anticipate, from the Greek *mousa*, meaning 'muse,' hence music, musical, musician.

A very long time ago some Sanskrit word-coiner determined that that thing now designated by 'mouse' was, in essence, a thieving thing. Semantic history went along with it: the mouse was, is, and will be, first and foremost, a criminal. A petty criminal, but a criminal nonetheless. And so, even when, enchanted, we read about the musical mouse, at some level we're denouncing it. 'Yes, a very pretty melody . . . but who did that *popcorn* belong to?'

Mus musculus. Guilty as charged. Poison, traps, and long, slow deaths.

The other night we heard a slap-pause-slap-pause and then a squeaking to wake the dead. It was the Ketch-All, newly positioned in a niche between the fridge and the basement door. It had not only caught two mice in one setting, it had caught two mice in *one minute*. Given the time of day, I figured that one of the mice was a Mr. Big. But who was the other? And what was all that squeaking? Blaming? Bullying? Biting? All I know is that it certainly wasn't singing. I listened and listened but there was not a to-wit-to-woo to be heard. I went downstairs and gave them the boot.

GERMAN COCKROACH (*Blatella germanica*)

NOBODY LIKES A COCKROACH. Look up 'cockroach' in the encyclopedia and you'll find the editors have lost their composure and let emotive adjectives such as 'disgusting' steal their way into the usual factual ramble. But I suppose they couldn't help themselves. It just seems human to dislike a cockroach.

The cockroaches that (saints be praised!) I *don't* have in my house at the moment are *Blatella germanica*, German cockroaches. When the slim, light brown, shiny scutters first infiltrated Europe from Africa they were called Prussian bugs by the Russians and Russian bugs by the Prussians. Nobody particularly wanted to lend them a piece of their national identity; but, perhaps owing to wars, the Germans got stuck—as deep in as Latin. Like house mice (and, for that matter, brown rats, bed bugs, and the new little mussel that's clogging up the Great Lakes), German cockroaches came to the New World on ships from the Old. Americans sometimes call German roaches 'Croton bugs' because they first started showing up in unsettling numbers in 1890 when the Croton Reservoir was tapped to augment New York City's water supply. It seems that hosts of cockroaches had been sitting in the dark Croton damp, tapping their hairy tarsi, waiting to get out.

WILD CULTURE

That's one of the 'problems' humans have with cockroaches; one of the reasons we so dislike them. When you see a cockroach sprint down the drain, you always have a feeling that there's a lot more where *that* came from—Down There. And you're right. In Minneapolis, a sewer compartment thirteen metres square was found to contain more than three thousand roaches.

Another problem with cockroaches is their durability. They never say die. A cockroach can live for months on little more than dust. A cockroach *with no head* can live for days. Cockroaches, in fact, could write the book on survival—they are the oldest insects we have. Their fossils date back to the carboniferous period (when a lot of coal was being formed), 300 or so million years ago. There's one sub-period, called the Pennsylvanian, whose strata have been found to contain so many cockroach fossils that its popular nickname among archeologists is 'The Age of Cockroaches'—an age I'm glad to have missed.

The adhesive pads that roaches have on their legs allow them to walk straight up windows, bathtubs, computer screens. But I suspect that, unlike most of their features, these pads could be improved upon, for my experience of cockroaches is that they tend to *drop* unexpectedly, particularly from the hanging lamp above the kitchen table. As they eat anything from crayons to boot leather to the machine oil in tape decks, they do tend to get into things (a problem) and their saliva contains a chemical that makes those things smell, well, cockroachy (another problem).

But however invasive they are, the idea that they carry disease has now apparently been discounted. Which is just as well. Howard Ensign Evans, in his book *Life on a Little-Known Planet*, quotes an entomologist who travelled through western Canada in 1903:

> Cockroaches thrive in British Columbia, as they do almost everywhere . . . They are in everything, even the food. On this trip I had them served to me in three different styles: alive in strawberries, à la carte with fried fish, and baked in biscuit.

The female German cockroach has an advantage over other bugs in that she can deposit her eggs at the last possible moment. She carries them around in a leathery case that she doesn't drop until the eggs are ready to hatch. That means there's less time for defenceless eggs to sit on the kitchen floor and be swept or vacuumed up, or to be eaten by something with that proclivity. When the eggs do hatch, the nymphs (miniatures of their parents) are off and running.

And that's a big problem. You open a cupboard door or turn on a light and cockroaches scatter like they've been up to no good. Cockroaches look guilty.

But, like I keep telling myself, all of these 'problems' with cockroaches are *ours*, really. And they're certainly not going to be solved by waging a chemical war (if such one-sided hostility can be called 'war'). They are problems to be thought about quietly, in a room with no distractions—particularly of the *Blatella* type. And that being the case, it's important to know how to keep roaches away, if you don't have them, and how to get them away, if you do. Well, I'm afraid the first thing to do is *clean*. There's nothing a cockroach likes less than a grease-free floor or crumb-free counter. The odd borax-baking soda treatment down the sink should help too.

Admittedly, though, sometimes cleaning is not enough. For instance, if you happen to live above a restaurant or grocery, you'll find that cockroaches will use your spanking clean apartment as a place in which to think about their own problems before heading back down-pipe to suck on the salad oil. So you'll need help. I've come across a number of possibilities. Cucumber is said to 'disagree' with cockroaches, although I'm not sure how you're to go about applying it. Putty is also supposed to be off-putting and, if you have the time and determination, will serve doubly as a way of stopping up all those incoming cockroach holes. You might have a toad, hedge-hog, or scorpion in your home—a natural, though naturally violent, deterrent. Or you might try the time-honoured treatment of holding a mirror up to the cockroach, which will so frighten it that it will never want to see your house again.

My favourite, though, is a method that was fashionable in Victorian England, where dislike of cockroaches was tempered by a sort of wistfulness. It's described in Frank Cowan's *Curious Facts in the History of Insects* (1865):

> It is no other than to address these pests a written letter containing the following words, or to this effect: 'O, Roaches, you have troubled me long enough, go now and trouble my neighbours.' It is well to write legibly and punctuate according to rule. ◉

FEAR OF KNOWING
IN MINNEAPOLIS

A place where wild is not chaos

IN BRIAN FAWCETT'S BOOK, *Public Eye: An Investigation into the Disappearance of the World,* he refers to a strict practice of the Dominican monks: they never embark on a discussion without first defining their terms. This seems like wise advice. If perchance you and I and a few others we know were to publish a little thing called *The Pamphlet of Wild Culture,* wouldn't we be wise as monks to first define what 'wild culture' is? Certainly that would be a sensible approach, but it raises another question that some might think is frivolous: Must we *know* what we're doing? And what is *knowing,* anyway? (Oh dear. I swear I didn't plan this. Can't stop now.)

At a conference I attended in Minneapolis called 'Early Warnings: Environment and the Media,' organized by Eric Utne and the Readers, I managed to speak to Utne himself, a lanky, midwestern, Jimmy Stewart-of-a-man. Judging by his magazine, which publishes the best of the alternative press, I felt Utne would have a keen sense of what distinguishes one alternative magazine from another; and after all, a good review of JWC appeared in *Utne Reader.* So, when I saw him standing alone for a millisecond, I darted in, hoping he might be able to give me the elegant yet earthy aphorism we had so feverishly searched for to define our magazine—the descriptive jewel that I could smuggle back over the Canadian border to use in a direct mail campaign that would go to every household in the free world, eliciting an unprecedented 100 percent response. Inspired by the patented Eric

Utne definition of our magazine, not one person who received our package would be able to resist subscribing for the maximum seven years. As I nervously approached the man who earlier that evening had been described as 'the Donald Trump of the Left,' beads of socially responsible, not-for-profit sweat dripped from my forehead, splashing quietly upon the polyester carpet at my feet. Face to face with him, I introduced myself and we shook hands. 'Ah, yes,' he said. 'The Journal of Wild Culture. Your magazine is . . . indescribable.'

Indescribable?!

Internally bruised, pain blinding me, I tried to regain my balance. Indescriba-ba-bable? Was that a compliment? Could we put that on the cover of our next issue? Could we win an award for The Most Outstanding Indescribable Magazine? Or more to the point, in this world of knowing where you're at and how you got there, was indescribable a sign of being flaky, without direction and potency, without an organized, relevant purpose? 'Gulp. Did it mean we were weak?

'It's been a pleasure to m-m-mate with you, Mr. Stewart,' I said as I shrunk into the carpet. There amid giant cigarette ashes, bits of hotel food and coffee-stained threads of Fortrel big as trees, I pondered 'indescribability.' I was hurt and lonely. No one was around to say, 'Hey, it's okay. Don't worry, man! Indescribable is hip! Who wants to be rigid, anyway. Indescribable is, well, *indescribable!* Don't get your pants in a knot!' I couldn't help it though, my pants were cutting off the circulation to my head. I looked out into this jungle of man-made fibres and felt dizzy and sick. How could I go back up there, up into that buzzing vestibule of publishers and editors of describable magazines, where, at any moment I might be asked the insidious, punishing question: What is The Journal of Wild Culture, anyway?

I couldn't. I could only slump onto the hard itchy rope weave of the jungle floor. Around me, the earth trembled. A sizzling Marlboro torch blazed through the sky into my flammable, machine-spun world. Its tainted embers ignited the enchanted Fortrel, turning it into fluid, choking goo. Pulling myself on my stomach under the purple flames, I used a *Squeezee Cheez*-smeared croissant flake to shield me from the fatal gases. There was only one way out. I knew I had to bring my world into focus with some kind of editorial statement. With a shard of graphite and a bit of chewed fingernail to write on, I tried to describe it . . .

The Journal of Wild Culture is a quarterly magazine for those interested in ecological issues from an artistic perspective—mind mulch, cranium compost, head humus. Articles include essays and features on a wide variety of subjects, with special focus on new ideas in ecology and its politics, bioregionalism, gender issues, organic and city-dweller gardening, cuisine using wild and organic foods, and oblique views of culture. The broadest possible definition of ecology* is explored in fiction, poetry, photography, pictorial essays by visual artists, and anything with humour that can guide us through the modern maze.

There is no line that determines the editorial perimeter of The *Journal of Wild Culture*. Boundaries are fluid. As we discover new paths that lead from the first one we followed, and as our writers, artists, and readers contribute their own ideas of what wild culture is, the periphery of the circle gets wider and wider.

While *The Journal of Wild Culture* and its parent organization, The Society for the Preservation of Wild Culture, are based in the Great Lakes bioregion and their activities encourage the discovery of the sense of this place, we hope that by being involved with us our readers and contributors from other areas will find the sense of place where they live.

If there is a philosophy in *The Journal of Wild Culture*, it is the search for values that could be, though are not now, at the heart of our culture. This search takes us into all areas of study and is informed by the notion that our imaginative and spiritual perception of the world is at least equal in importance to our intellectual and scientific

*ECOLOGY IS 'THE RELATIONSHIP OF ORGANISMS TO EACH OTHER AND THEIR ENVIRONMENT'; IN GREEK, ECOLOGY MEANS 'THE STUDY OF THE HOUSEHOLD.'

knowledge. *The Journal of Wild Culture* can therefore be seen as a kind of manual for the reinvention of the world.

Finally, wild is not chaos. On the contrary, it is perfection if there is any, the perfect order between the rational and the irrational—Nature's internal agreement with itself. And, like soil, wild is self-regulating and interdependent. *The Journal of Wild Culture* evolved as a forum for that agreement, where playfulness and authority harmonize, where there is a tolerance for ambiguity and a commitment to cultivating what never grows the same way twice.

I suddenly found myself with my feet firmly planted on the ground. There were no cigarette burns in the carpet, nor was anyone smoking. The hotel lobby was a cleaner place than I had thought, and Eric Utne no longer looked like Jimmy Stewart. In fact, nothing looked like anything else I'd ever seen in my life before. It was all new and indescribable and I didn't mind . . . anything. The jungle was quiet.

There was no fear and there was no knowing.

MEREDITH ANDREW is a writer, editor, and pool hall attendant. She now spends as much time as possible in her garden, digging up new things to write about.

DAVID CAYLEY produces radio documentaries for CBC Radio IDEAS. He is the author of *The Age of Ecology* (Lorimer, 1991), *Northrop Frye in Conversation*, and *Ivan Illich in Conversation* (Anansi 1992).

THOMAS A. CLARK is an English poet who lives on Rockness Hill in a place called Nailsworth. A book of his short poems entitled, *Madder Lake*, is available from Coach House Press, Toronto.

CHRISTOPHER DEWDNEY is a poet and neurotic whose most recent book of poetry, Book III of *A Natural History of Southern Ontario*, is published by The Figures in Massachusetts.

PAUL DUTTON is a performer, musician, and writer. His recent publications are *Additives, Aurealities, Visionary Portraits*.

BRAHM EILEY is a writer and satirist with an interest in political economy and popular culture. He enjoys walks in the London fog and looking for trouble.

BRIAN FAWCETT is a writer, editor, and author of many books including *Unusual Circumstances, Interesting Times* (Harper Collins, 1992) and *The Compact Gardener* (Firefly, 1992).

JOHN FERGUSON is an architect who has two daughters, two jobs, and two left feet. He enjoys living in the city.

GARDENESQUE is the *nom de plume* of Juliet Mannock, a gardener, writer, and arts program organizer for CBC TV's "Sunday Arts Entertainment."

SUE GELINAS is a poet who works as a technical writer in Los Angeles. In her spare time she teaches her dog to look like a moose.

(continued)

HANK HEDGES is a retired educator, television host, and author who lives on a farm near the Niagara Escarpment. In 1983 he was nominated Educator of the Year in Ontario.

MARNI JACKSON'S work has appeared in magazines such as Saturday Night, Maclean's and Rolling Stone. Her most recent book is *The Mother Zone* (MacFarlane, Walter & Ross, 1992).

STEVEN KLINE, a Professor of Communications at Simon Fraser University, is the author of *Out of the Garden: Children in the Age of Marketing* (Verso, 1992). His interest in Enilk Nevets began when, as a young boy, he first saw his own name reflected in a mirror.

BPNICHOL, a well-loved Canadian poet and essayist, died at the age of 44 in 1988. He is best known for his *Martyrology* series and his work as a founding member of the sound-poetry group, The Four Horsemen.

MARILYN POWELL is a writer and radio producer at CBC program, *Ideas*. She holds a doctorate in Medieval Literature from Harvard.

RICHARD PURDY is a Montreal-based pataphysician and visual artist specializing in invented artifacts and cultures including *The Inversion of the World*, *Corpus Christi*, and *Lucifer*.

SARAH SHEARD is an editor and writer of fiction and non-fiction. Her first novel, *Almost Japanese*, has appeared in eight foreign editions. Her second novel, *The Swing Era*, is scheduled to appear in the spring of 1993 from Knopf Canada.

MERLIN STONE is a New York-based writer and historian whose 1976 study, *When God Was a Woman*, helped to trigger contemporary efforts to recover the history and wisdom of the Great Goddess.

TIM WILSON is a broadcaster and writer specializing in experimental and cross-cultural sound. He recently produced the audio tape, *Man and the Wild Child* (Boulder: Soundstrue, 1992). ◉

ACKNOWLEDGEMENTS

THE EDITORS would like to thank Alicia Peres and Marie Patterson for their time and care in the production of this collection.

Since its first issue in 1987, *The Journal of Wild Culture* has been created by many people in addition to those whose work is reprinted in this book. We would like to thank everyone who has contributed to the writing, illustration, editing and design of the magazine, and to the ongoing life of the Society for the Preservation of Wild Culture through its readings, cafés, board meetings, and auctions.

In roughly chronological order, we would like to mention (for their wit, talent and tolerance for ambiguity) Kim Obrist, Peter Ferguson, Patricia Beatty, Judith Fitzgerald, Gary Michael Dault, Leslie McAllister, Karen Mulhallen, Barbara Klunder, Peter Scargall, Cathy Smith, Hank Hedges, Henry Rodriguez, Bruce MacDonald, David Cayley, Leonard Knott, Rob Glen, Brian Fawcett, Jenny Fraser, Christopher Dewdney, Michael Stadtlander, Brenda Darling, Tim Wilson, Arthur Gelgoot & Associates, Chris Loudon, Les Bowser, Rita Davies, Marcia Rioux, Bill Peden, Frank Addario, Jean Riley, Judy MacDonald, Duncan Kennedy, Tom Skudra, Bernie Lucht, Gar Smith, Allan Sparrow, Marni Jackson, Vicky Elsom, Bettina Scargall, David Young, Terry McGlade, David Spence, Francis Stober, Claire Ironside, Diana Bryden, Julia Blushak, Bob Wilcox, Rick/Simon, Tim Gould, Caroline Sneath, Susan O'Neil, Don Houston, Roberta Pazdro, Yvonne Bayer, Jack Layton, Avril Orloff, Peter Herrndorf, Marq de Villiers, Marc Glassman, Michael Ruehle, Andrea Malenkovich, John Ferguson, David Warren, John Knechtel, June Callwood, Liz White, Marie Lou Rowley, Nijole Mockevicius, Barbara Gowdy, Robert France, Janette Platana, Denise Marcella, Glenna Munro, Peter Commins, Richard Levine, Marien Lewis, Cynthia Rathwell, Jamie Kennedy, Sharon Hall, Mary Ovenstone, Lucy White, Lynna Landstreet, Kerry Quinlan, Mark Howell, Jens Köhler, Lisa Nabiezsko, Drora Tene, David Levine, Clari Felke and Peter Berg.

Not us, but the wind that blows through us.